Advance Accolades for *The Class Meeting* . . .

Dr. Kevin Watson has given every church and pastor a gift! The gift is the reclaiming of the Wesley Class Meeting as the primary disciple growing tool. Any church willing to use this book as a guide will experience what I experienced at Christ Church United Methodist in Ft. Lauderdale, Florida. I was there when Wesley Fellowship Groups began and I had the honor to watch an outpouring of the Holy Spirit. If this is a hunger in your heart, then this book by Dr. Watson will be a must-read for you.

Richard J. Wills, Jr.
Bishop UMC, retired

Kevin Watson has given a wonderful gift for our church. He has resurrected an historic Wesleyan practice—the class meeting—and has given it fresh meaning, showing its relevance for the church today. Kevin shows us how the class meeting may be a perfect means for church renewal, a gift of God, through the Wesleyan movement, for such a time as this.

Will Willimon
Bishop UMC, retired
Professor of the Practice of Christian Ministry
Duke Divinity School

Dr. Kevin Watson's emphasis upon renewing the Methodist movement takes a pragmatic approach. The intent of this book is to be practiced, not merely read.

Tom Harrison
Senior Pastor
Asbury United Methodist Church
Tulsa, Oklahoma

This powerful practice must be reclaimed, but not just for adults, for all ages. Do your youth pastor a favor and give him/her a copy of this deeply rooted and thoroughly practical book!

Jeremy W. Steele
Next Generation Minister
Christ United Methodist Church
Mobile, Alabama

Kevin Watson's new book is a clarion call to recover the Methodist class meeting as a vital means of grace with an eye on the renewal of the church in the twenty-first century. Rightly balancing the historical and the practical, Watson invites readers to embrace not only the generous value of the class meeting in the past but also to participate in what promise it holds for the present and beyond in raising up disciples of Jesus Christ.

Kenneth J. Collins
Professor of Historical Theology and Wesley Studies
Asbury Theological Seminary

Kevin Watson has written a fresh new guide to the theory and practice of the Wesley Class meeting, an essential element of truly Wesleyan spirituality. As an experienced participant and initiator of class meetings in academic and congregational settings, Watson is a faithful guide. I highly recommend this book to clergy and congregations who are looking for ways to develop deeper discipleship and reconnect with our own rich Wesleyan heritage.

Elaine A. Heath, Ph.D.
Southern Methodist University
Cofounder, the Missional Wisdom Foundation
Director, the Academy for Missional Wisdom

As the United Methodist Church struggles to redefine itself and its mission for the next generation of disciples, Kevin Watson has managed to reconnect us to a timeless practice that has the potential of "revitalizing" our denomination—the class meeting! With so much emphasis on declining membership and loss of relevancy, we are invited to rediscover what made Methodism and the Wesleyan movement so vibrant for over a century.

Could it be that we've been looking in all the wrong places for the right answers? Watson reminds us that the class meeting is not an end in itself, but it has the ability to bring together and transform core groups of people who "are willing to invest in each other's lives and who are desperate to grow in their relationship with Jesus."

What I treasure most about this book is the way Watson traces the history of the class meeting, shares the basics of what should/should not take place within the group, and defines for us the role and qualities of the class leader. In other words, this is *not* a history book that simply tells us what happened *then*. Instead, it is a modern-day road map that points us in the direction of what *can* happen *now*!

If you are one of those Christians seeking to experience the height, depth, length, width, and breadth of God's purpose and meaning for your life, you need to know you can discover it in a place we've yet to look—the class meeting!

Robert E. Hayes Jr.
Bishop UMC

We want to know and be known. We need to hear each other's stories. Watson's compelling case for reinventing the Methodist class meeting recognizes that holy living must be rooted in confession, accountable community, testimony, and gentle shepherding.

Stan Ingersol, Ph.D.
Denominational Archivist, Church of the Nazarene

Like other key aspects of Christian living, the Wesleyan class meeting is often talked about today but seldom really practiced. For Wesley, the class meeting included, but was much more than, "small-group fellowship."

Kevin Watson understands this, and he writes out of both research and personal experience. The strength of authentic Wesleyanism is that it denies the sharp distinction between head knowledge and heart experience. Rather, it unites them. We find that strength here in this practical book.

To be effective today, the class meeting must be recontextualized (that is, made workable) without losing its essential dynamic as gospel-based accountable community. I commend this book as a useful tool that, if put into practice, can achieve that goal.

Howard A. Snyder, PhD
Author, *The Radical Wesley and Patterns for Church Renewal*

Kevin Watson gives us living proof and examples of the transformational power of small groups that carry the unique DNA of Methodism. If you only intend to read and discuss this book, you will miss the point altogether and might actually end up in hell.* If you prayerfully enter into this Wesleyan experience for eight weeks, you will prepare yourself for heaven. (*Hell in this context means the place of perpetual reading and discussion with no real or lasting change, transformation, spiritual growth, or maturity.)

Tom Albin
Dean of The Upper Room Ministries
and Ecumenical Relations
General Board of Discipleship
The United Methodist Church

THE CLASS MEETING

THE CLASS MEETING

Reclaiming a Forgotten
(and Essential)
Small Group Experience

KEVIN M. WATSON

 seedbed

To Bethany, James, and Eden

Contents

Preface   xiii

Acknowledgments   xvii

1. A New (Old) Kind of Small Group   3

2. The Class Meeting: The Heart of the Methodist Revival   19

3. Moving into God's House: The Theological Foundation
   of the Class Meeting   35

4. Becoming Wesleyan Again   53

5. The Basics: From Start to Finish   77

6. The Role of the Class Leader   93

7. What Could Possibly Go Wrong?   111

8. The Keys to a Life-Changing Group   129

A Concluding Exhortation   145

Notes   149

Preface

This is a book that has been on my mind for a long time. For years I have felt that a recovery of the class meeting in the contemporary church would be used by the Holy Spirit as a renewing means of grace. When I began writing and speaking about the early Methodist class meeting, particularly in local church contexts, I was surprised at how quick many people were to accept my argument that the class meeting was a key piece of early Methodist vitality and that it has something to offer us today. I was even more surprised at how quickly people turned to very practical questions: How would you reinstitute class meetings today? How often should they meet? How long should each meeting be? What is the role of the leader?

I became convinced of two things that led me to write this book in its current form. First, there is strong interest and desire in many parts of the Wesleyan/Methodist family to reclaim the class meeting. Second, Wesleyan/Methodist communities have, for the most part, moved so far away from this practice that these groups will mostly need to be started from scratch. As a result, this book seeks to provide an introduction to the class meeting that will enable local churches to reclaim this practice. No prior knowledge of the class meeting, or even general small group dynamics, is expected. This is intended to be a guide for beginners, though I certainly hope it will also be useful to people with more experience with small groups.

The primary way I envision this book being used is as a way to jump-start class meetings. The book is designed to be used as an eight-week study that gradually shifts from an informational study about the class meeting to a class meeting itself. The goal of this book is to enable people to continue meeting as a class. In other words, my deep hope is that after the eight weeks are over, the group will continue meeting, simply following the basic format of the class meeting. To this end, each chapter has a guide for small group discussion at the end. The guide provides both questions for discussion and a "Transformation Question," which is intended to help people gain comfort with talking about the state of their souls, and build a vocabulary for doing so. The first few weeks, the discussion is primarily centered on the content of the chapter. However, over the course of the study, more time is given to discussing the Transformation Question, which also becomes more focused each week. Over the eight weeks of the study, the group is being prepared to become a class meeting. For me, it would be a failure if a small group used this book as a study about the class meeting and then simply moved on to another study.

The book can also be used as a resource for local church leaders, either pastors or laity, as a handbook for starting class meetings. The book can help leaders make the case for why class meetings are important, as well as think through the practical details of how to start a class meeting from nothing, how to identify a class leader, and how to conduct the weekly meeting. In other words, one could read this book to learn about the history and dynamics of the class meeting and then use it to help a small group become a class meeting.

The first part of the book (chapters 1–4) provides a theoretical introduction to the class meeting. Chapter 1 argues that though there are many different types of small groups, they are not equally effective at helping people grow in their faith in Jesus. Chapter 2 provides a brief historical introduction to the Methodist Revival and the key role class meetings played in the revival. Chapter 3 provides a basic introduction to Wesleyan theology, describing the theological foundation of the early Methodist class meeting. And chapter 4 narrates the decline of the class meeting and discusses why this approach to small groups is essential for contemporary Christianity.

The second part of the book (chapters 5–8) provides a practical guide to starting and developing class meetings. Chapter 5 outlines the basics of the class meeting, including how to start a class meeting in a church where there are none at all. Chapter 6 describes the strategic role of the class leader. Chapter 7 discusses common obstacles to a successful class meeting, as well as ways to prevent these common pitfalls from harming your group. Finally, chapter 8 narrates the keys to a life-changing small group.

I wrote this book because I believe the Holy Spirit wants to use this particular approach to small groups to bring renewal to the lives of women and men created in the image of God. My prayer is that you will find participating in a class meeting to be a means of God's transforming grace in your life.

May it be so! Amen.

Acknowledgments

This book is the result of sustained interest over several years in a practical guide to reclaiming the early Methodist class meeting. While it is up to the reader to determine whether this book successfully provides such a guide, I would like to express my gratitude to the various audiences who convinced me of the need for this book. During my first semester as a PhD student at Southern Methodist University, I met a small group of students at Perkins School of Theology who wanted more intentional Christian formation during their time in seminary. We formed a weekly class meeting, which was a blessing to me during my three years in Dallas. I am also particularly grateful to the following communities that helped me refine my thinking about the class meeting while I was in Dallas: Andy Roberts and the Southern Methodist University Wesley Foundation; McFarlin United Methodist Church in Norman, Oklahoma; and Nexus Community within Richardson Church of the Nazarene in Richardson, Texas.

I am thankful for the comments and questions that my writing on the class meeting and its ongoing value for contemporary Christianity have received on my blog, as well as on Twitter and Facebook. Thank you to all who have not only read my writing, but have taken the time to thoughtfully and charitably respond. And thank you to all who have made time to talk with me about these ideas in person or by phone. I am particularly grateful to Jeremiah Hinton, who read an early draft of the manuscript and offered helpful feedback.

Two speaking invitations especially spurred me to start writing about the class meeting. I am grateful to have been invited to lead a breakout session at the Scripture as Formation conference at Seattle Pacific University and to have been invited to be the keynote speaker for the meeting of the Virginia Society for Wesleyan Studies in the fall of 2011. Both audiences were attentive and gracious, while asking piercing questions that have shaped this book.

I am also grateful for the Spiritual and Education Resources for Vocational Exploration (SERVE) grants I received from Seattle Pacific University to direct a pilot project that gave me the opportunity to implement class meetings in an undergraduate setting. I appreciate the expert guidance and encouragement Margaret Diddams provided, as well as the support Douglas M. Strong provided for this project as the dean in the School of Theology. The project would not have been possible without the faculty who agreed to participate: Jeffrey Keuss, Michael D. Langford, and J. J. Johnson Leese. And thanks, of course, are due to the students who participated in these class meetings.

The idea of "watching over one another in love" is not my own. I am deeply aware that I am standing on the shoulders of giants. I thank God for the legacies of Philipp Jakob Spener, Anthony Horneck, John and Charles Wesley, and the many others before and since who have given Christians well-worn paths to follow. I am also thankful to all who have more recently invested their time and energy in lifting up the value of this practice, especially David Lowes Watson and Steven W. Manskar. I also thank John Meunier and Nick Weatherford, who kindly gave me permission to quote comments from my blog in this book. Bishop Dick Wills graciously spent a significant amount of time talking with me about the way "Wesley Fellowship Groups" worked at Christ United Methodist Church in Fort Lauderdale, Florida, when he was the senior pastor.

I am also thankful for the investment that Seedbed has made in this book. Their immediate enthusiasm for this project and their emphatic agreement on the need to reclaim the class meeting reflect the kind of investment from a publisher for which any author would be grateful. Holly Jones was a wonderful production director. This book is also better because of the attention given to it by the copy editor Renee Chavez; the page designer and typesetter Kristin Goble at PerfecType; the cover designer, Nick Perreault; and the proofreaders, Amanda Sauer and Bill Fentum. Thanks are especially due to Andrew Miller and J. D. Walt, who both read the book at various stages with care, were unfailingly patient with me, and offered encouragement throughout the writing process.

Finally, I thank my family. My parents have been a constant and unfailing source of love and support. I am blessed to be married to Melissa. More than anyone else's, her love, support, and encouragement have made this book possible. If not for her, it would never have been written. She often joined me at the kitchen table when I was writing after our kids were in bed, and she never complained about frequent interruptions of her reading with the incessant questions authors ask when they are in the midst of writing or editing and have a captive audience. Melissa, thank you for always staying at the table with me! And to my children, Bethany, James, and Eden, I will always love you. This book is dedicated to you, with the prayer that the Holy Spirit will provide you with the kind of community described in these pages and that it will help you grow in your love and knowledge of the One who loves you even more than I do.

THE
CLASS
MEETING

1

A New (Old) Kind of Small Group

We have no doubt, but meetings of christian brethren for the exposition of scripture-texts, may be attended with their advantages. But the most profitable exercise of any is a free inquiry into the state of the heart.[1]

—Francis Asbury and Thomas Coke

What Is a Small Group?

Small groups may be one of the most frequently endorsed and least understood pieces of the Christian life. A Google search of the phrase "small groups" retrieved a ridiculous 21 million results. A search of the same phrase from the books listed on Amazon.com yielded 16,296 results.[2] And yet, despite the amount of information about small groups, I often find myself scratching my head when reading about small groups. Does anyone really know what a small group is? Is it simply a group that is small?

A recent study sought to identify what factors are most important to congregational vitality. The study found that one of the key "drivers" of vitality was the number of small groups.[3] Initially, I was thrilled (though not surprised) to see that small groups were so visibly recognized as key to the vitality of a congregation. This is, after all, widely recognized by pastors. Large churches will often talk about how small groups helped them grow larger by becoming smaller. Yet, studies like the one just cited often have either very vague definitions of "small group" or no definition at all. What does it really mean to say that the number of small groups is a factor in the vitality of a congregation, particularly if there is no definition of what a small group is? Here is one example of why this matters:

Not too long ago, a church had a campaign to start new small groups. The church advertised the drive each week in the Sunday morning bulletin and in the church newsletter. Members of the church were asked to think about what type of small group they might like to join. The results of this project were telling. New small groups were started; however, none of the groups had any explicit emphasis on Christian faith. Most surprising to me was the formation of a "Red Hat Society." If you don't know what these groups are, I will just say that they do not appear to have much of anything to do with Christian formation, though they do have something to do with wearing red hats (look it up). While I certainly hope that this church is an exception and not the rule, it made me wonder if the key factors in successfully starting new small groups are low Christian commitment and hobbies that members already have. If the vision for small groups is this shallow, how can they be considered a driver of congregational vitality? Is there a difference between the body of Christ and a social club with people in it? I believe that there is and that we must cast a more robust vision for small groups within a Christian context.

Not all small groups are created equal! Some small groups are better than others.

As I have interacted with various approaches to small groups, I would say that there are three main approaches to small groups in contemporary Christianity. First, there are affinity groups. These groups are organized around common passions, interests, or hobbies. Examples would be: a cooking club, a bowling league, or a book club. The small group campaign previously mentioned ended up starting affinity groups. While the desire to participate in such a group is not bad, this is not what I mean by a small group within a Christian context. Furthermore, I think they should be the lowest priority of a Christian church's small group ministry, as they are the least effective in helping people become disciples of Jesus Christ.

Information-driven groups comprise the second type of small groups. These groups are focused on conveying information and are organized by a common curriculum. Examples would be: Sunday school, a Bible study, or a study of any other book or curriculum. In these groups, members gather together to learn more about their faith. An assumption of these groups is that knowledge is essential for maturity of faith, or that right living is dependent on right knowing. In my experience, this is the kind of group most people have in mind when they think about a small group. At their best, these groups push participants to apply what they are learning to their lives. At their worst, they can be poorly conceived and organized and have no impact on the way group members actually live. Ultimately, I think there is a role for small groups that study curriculum in Christian settings. Biblical literacy and awareness of basic Christian doctrine are important for faithful Christian living. However, information-driven small groups are *not* the most effective way to help people become mature Christians.

The third type of small groups are transformation-driven groups. These groups focus not on discussion or mastery of content, but on changed lives, on group members' experience of God. These small groups are organized around a common desire to support one another in their efforts to become increasingly faithful Christians who are growing in love of God and neighbor. Examples would be: accountability groups, fellowship groups, cell groups, class meetings, and perhaps even house churches. These groups are primarily focused on living and not on learning. They are especially focused on being made new by the grace of God, not only on receiving new ideas about God. These groups consist of people who want to more effectively practice their faith. This book argues that *it is these types of groups that are the most effective at making disciples of Jesus Christ, and as a result, churches should be the most invested in establishing, promoting, and nurturing them.*

In fact, this book is an introduction to one particular group in this category, the class meeting. A class meeting is a small group that is primarily focused on transformation and not information, where people learn how to interpret their entire lives through the lens of the gospel, build a vocabulary for giving voice to their experience of God, and grow in faith in Christ. Class meetings were the most important and most basic practice of early Methodists, which was one of the fastest-growing movements of Christianity in America. So what happened to class meetings? This question will be further explored in chapter 4, but for now it will suffice to say that Methodists became addicted to curriculum and gradually turned to information-driven small groups and away from the class meeting.

Addicted to Curriculum

Over the past several decades there have been some poor quality small group studies published; however, there have also been some exceptional studies that are well conceived, well written, and designed with maximum forethought. One of the best recent examples of the latter is *Disciple: Becoming Disciples Through Bible Study*.[4] *Disciple* is a thirty-four-week study that requires deep commitment from participants. I have witnessed the effectiveness of *Disciple* both firsthand and at a distance. It does the best job of any curriculum-driven approach to small groups that I have seen. In fact, *Disciple* self-consciously strives to bridge the gap between informational and transformational approaches to the Christian life. As the title of the first book in the series suggests, a major conviction of *Disciple* is that discipleship happens through studying the Bible. In *Disciple*, participants read significant passages of Scripture during the week, as well as a study guide that helps them think about these readings. During the small group time, the participants watch a movie clip, discuss key themes of the reading, and challenge one another to apply what they have read to their lives. I would be willing to go so far as to say that *Disciple* does this better than any other study that I know of. And yet, as good as *Disciple* is, it is still primarily a curriculum-driven study. And its success actually illustrates one of the tendencies of information-driven approaches to small groups more clearly.

Curriculum can become addicting. The deeper question for Christian leaders is: Which form of small group experience is most effective at helping people become disciples of Jesus Christ: an informational small group primarily focused on content and that asks questions of application as time allows, or a transformation focused small group that provides space for the participants to wrestle with the particularities of what is going on in their lives with Christ (like the class meeting)?

From my perspective, the more time Christians spend on curriculum-based studies, the more dependent they become on them. Instead of releasing Christians to love God and neighbor with their lives, curriculum often seems to make people feel less confident in their own ability to understand and respond to unexpected circumstance in their lives. Ask yourself a question: What did you do the last time you were particularly earnest in your desire to grow in your faith? Did you ask someone you perceived to be an expert to recommend a book? I know that I have often asked that question, and when I was the pastor of a church, these types of questions were the ones I was most frequently asked.

But the Christian life is not primarily about *knowing* the right things. It is about *living in Christ*. Christians, particularly those who are predisposed to participate in a small group, often already know a lot. In fact, many Christians know far more than they practice. Christian discipleship, then, is more like an apprenticeship to Jesus Christ than it is about mastering a body of knowledge. Jesus came so that we could have abundant life, not merely so that we could have the right ideas about who he is. Class meetings provide a format that helps people actively grow in their faith in Christ together in community, not just study information.

At this stage, let me clarify that I am not saying that information or ideas are irrelevant. Some ways of talking about Jesus are better than others. In fact, some are wholly inadequate and should be rejected by Christians. Doctrine matters. It is essential. Christians should be introduced to and taught sound doctrine. And yet, as important as Christian doctrine is in informing the Christian life, it was never intended to be an end in itself. Doctrine provides boundaries and direction that can help one discern what they ought to do and what they should not do. It provides necessary guidelines for living the Christian life, but one still has to actually begin living such a life! Moreover, many informational approaches to the Christian life aren't even focused on doctrine, they are primarily focused on life strategies, self-help guidelines (and often you could come to the same conclusions these books come to without the "Christian" content), or basic mapping of the content of Scripture.

Class Meetings Promote Active Faith

In class meetings, however, participants actively discuss the state of their current relationship with God and how they are living out (and sometimes failing to live out) their faith. In curriculum-driven small groups, participants are in a passive posture, receiving information that is given to them through the book that is being studied, or through the leader, who is the expert. One of the common bonds of the group is the curriculum that is at the center of the group. In this way, curriculum can provide helpful focus and organization to the group (the group can literally be "on the same page"). On the other hand, curriculum distances the participants from their own lives. For people who feel a bit uncomfortable talking about their relationships with God, a study can be less intimidating because they can talk about the content instead of really talking about their relationship with God.

In many ways this is understandable. It can feel uncomfortably vulnerable to share with other people what is going on in your relationship with God. You may fear being ineloquent, not having something profound to say, or being judged by other members of your group. In contrast, a study is usually more straightforward. If you read the material and come to the group prepared, you can be relatively confident that you won't embarrass yourself. The problem is that these types of groups rarely act as a bridge to deeper and more meaningful conversations about the state of one's soul. In fact, I have had several encounters with people who have been a part of a Sunday school class (which is the grand experiment in the informational approach to Christian discipleship) for almost their whole lives. I hope I am wrong, but my experience has shown me that there is not necessarily a meaningful connection between faithful participation in Sunday school and maturity in Christian discipleship. Sunday school does not make saints, because (pardon the cliché) it is primarily focused on helping people talk the talk, but not walk the walk.

Let's use this book itself as an example. The goal of this book is to convince you to participate in a particular type of small group—a contemporary class meeting. The strategy for achieving this goal is to use a curriculum (this book) to study the class meeting and to gradually transition from a study to a class meeting. In other words, this is intended to be a resource that will help you join a small group where you, with others, learn how to increasingly filter every part of your life through the lens of the gospel, increase your ability to give voice to your experience of God's presence and action in your life, and grow in your faith in Christ. One of the ways this will be accomplished is through the organization of the small group time. In the discussion questions for each week, there will be questions about the chapter content and a question about your life with God. This question is designed to help you begin to risk sharing with other people how things are going in your walk with God. If you have not been in a group where you talked about your experience of God, the questions at the end of the study may initially make you a bit uncomfortable. You may even find yourself hoping there isn't enough time to get to the question that is focused on your life with God!

In this chapter, for instance, it might require less risk for you to talk about the difference between informational and transformational approaches to small groups than to actually enter into a conversation about how God has worked in your life through a particular form of small group. In this example, talking generally about the difference between various kinds of small groups is most representative of an informational approach to small groups. Talking about how God has worked in your life through a particular small group experience, on the other hand, is most representative of a transformational approach to small groups. And yet, convincing you of the value of transformational small groups is of little value if you do not decide to actually participate in such a group. What good would it do for me to convince you to join a group that was focused on your journey with God if you did not actually join such a group? Too often, studies focus on trying to convince participants that ideas are true without helping people live based on this newly discovered truth. Information-driven groups are most effective at the intellectual level. They do not do nearly as good a job leading to meaningful conversion, changed hearts, and changed lives. Class meetings are focused on precisely these things—how is the amazing grace of God changing your heart, your life, and your relationship with other people?

Let me put this more boldly: information-driven small groups that do not lead to a changed life are no more valuable for Christian discipleship than a weather report that does not impact the clothes you wear. If I turn on the Weather Channel and am told that there is a 90 percent chance of rain today, I will bring my rain jacket with me when I leave the house. This book hopes to help you form a class meeting, where you will actively pursue deeper faith in Christ with others. At times, participating in this group may stretch you a bit, because the group is about more than your ideas about Christianity. The group is about your relationship with Jesus, the Son of God. And Jesus does not want to change only our minds, or what we think; he wants to change our hearts and how we live. So, I hope you will take this step, because the history of early Methodism is a testament to the way the Holy Spirit has used the class meeting to help people come to know Jesus Christ more intimately.

The Goal of This Study

The goal of this study is twofold. First, I hope to convince you that a group like the early Methodist class meeting is the most important type of small group of which you could be a part. If you can only be in one small group, I hope to convince you to choose to be in a class meeting, because it is most likely to help you become a more faithful and more committed Christian. Yet, it would be an ironic failure if this book, above all books, only impacted your thoughts. The second goal of this book is to help you actually try out this kind of group. This book is both a study of the early Methodist class meeting and a gradual introduction to experiencing what it would be like to be in this kind of group. A guide for the small group time is provided for each week that has both discussion questions about the content of each chapter and one question that focuses on each person's experience of God. The goal is for these questions to stretch you a bit each week, so that by the end of the eight weeks, you will be ready to pursue Christ together in a class meeting. If you find the last question a bit intimidating, you can always read it before the group meeting so you have plenty of time to think about your answer.

My hope is that you will be willing to try this kind of group. The point is not that the class meeting has magical powers, or that it is the key to our salvation. Only Jesus can save us. The class meeting is valuable because participating in a group that asks you weekly how you are doing in your relationship with God is one of the most effective ways you can plan to stay focused on your growth as a follower of Jesus Christ. My own experience has repeatedly shown me that this is essential for my relationship with Christ. Many Christians who have gone before us have similarly testified that "watching over one another in love" has been of deep significance for their relationships with God.[5] This approach to small groups is also making a difference in the lives of many contemporary Christians. Here is one example: Nick Weatherford, a lay member of Munger Place Church[6] in Dallas,

Texas, has said of his initial experience with a class meeting and the impact it had on his faith:

> I have come to realize the importance of being called into community with one another and of God's unrelenting grace. We are not asked to, or intended to do this alone. I would argue from personal experience that our faith will wither away over time if we are not proactively involving ourselves in community with other believers.

> In contemporary churches, there seem to be ample opportunities for Bible studies and other programs, but it is much harder to find a group that is primarily focused on your relationship with God. Kitchen Groups (this is what we call our class meeting–like groups at Munger) don't follow any particular curriculum. We just ask you to analyze your own experiences through the lens of faith. What has God revealed to you this week? What do you need to work on? What is holding you back? It doesn't ask you to measure up to any particular standard other than a genuine desire to be more of who you are being called to be as a follower of Jesus.

> Kitchen Groups foster a community of honesty and personal accountability. The accountability comes not in any prescribed set of rules or confessions but in learning to understand and respond to all of our experiences, good and bad, through the perspective of our relationship with God. I think more about my faith than I ever have in my life, asking myself more and more often "How is my life in God?" even outside of the group setting.[7]

Ultimately, we cannot stand still or tread water in the Christian life. We are either moving closer toward God and learning to better love our neighbor, or we are missing opportunities to further express our love for God and neighbor and gradually moving away from God. The goal of every Christian should be to become a disciple, a follower, of Jesus Christ. People do not learn how to follow Jesus by reading books about following Jesus. We learn how to follow Jesus by following him, even if by fits and starts.

Many church leaders recognize that small groups are an invaluable tool for helping people learn how to follow Jesus. But again, *not all small groups are created equal.* The community that can be fostered through small group formation is a dynamic asset in helping people become more like Christ. This kind of community is created when people join together to support one another on their journeys, and when the journey itself is the focus of the community, not a book about the journey.

In the passage above, Nick testified to the importance of community for his own faith journey. As he gathered together with other Christians to talk about his life in God, he found not only that he learned how to better talk about his life in God during the group time, but also that this helped him to live out his faith in more and more of his life. My hope is that the Holy Spirit will use this book to help people who are seeking God learn how to bring themselves more fully to the Father, Son, and Holy Spirit and to support one another in this journey.

Guide for Small Group Discussion

At the end of each chapter, there will be a guide for the time spent together as a small group. The actual meeting should be an hour and fifteen minutes each week. The organization of the group will vary slightly from week to week as the group gradually moves away from a study of transformational small groups to *becoming* a transformational small group.

At the time the group is scheduled to start, the group leader should call the group together, thank everyone for coming, and open with a prayer. The next fifteen minutes should be spent providing the opportunity for group members to begin to get to know one another. Each participant should be invited to share their name, how long they have been involved in this church, and what made them interested in being a part of this group. (Leaders should feel free to use their common sense in adjusting these questions based on the dynamics of the group. For example, people don't need to introduce themselves if everyone already knows each other and this would be artificial.)

The next forty-five minutes should be spent discussing the content of the first chapter, using the "Questions for Discussion" as a guide to the discussion. (It is okay if you do not discuss all the questions. Feel free to dwell on one question as long as the conversation is lively and focused on the general theme of the chapter.)

The last fifteen minutes should be spent discussing the Transformation Question. The leader should keep track of the time and make sure that the discussion of the chapter is brought to a close in time to get to the last question, which is really the most important question for the week. (Leaders: It is okay if you can't think of a smooth transition from one topic to the next. You may simply say, for instance, "Now, I'd like us to shift our focus to our last question for tonight . . ." You should be prepared for the last question to perhaps make people a bit uncomfortable; there may be a bit of a tendency to try to filibuster, or run out the clock, to avoid the question. One of your most important jobs is to be willing to shift the conversation to this question.) It is important that every person has an opportunity to answer the question. Finally, the leader should close with a prayer.

Organization:

Open with a Prayer

:00–:15 Introductions

What is your name?

How long have you been involved in this church?

What made you interested in being a part of this study?

:15–1:00 Questions for Discussion

1. What were your general thoughts or reactions to this chapter? Was there anything particularly exciting or challenging to you? Why?

2. Discuss the strengths and weaknesses as you see them of the three types of small groups discussed at the beginning of this chapter (affinity groups, information-driven groups, and transformation-driven groups).

3. Of these three types of small groups, which one do you have the most previous experience with? Describe what this group did well and what it may not have done well.

4. Do you agree that groups that are focused on transformation are likely to be most effective in making disciples of Jesus Christ? Why or why not?

1:00–1:15 Transformation Question

On a scale of 1 to 10 (1 being the farthest you have ever felt from God, 10 being the closest you have ever felt to God) what number would you give to how close you feel to God today? Why?

Close with a Prayer

2

The Class Meeting: The Heart of the Methodist Revival

Never omit meeting your Class or Band . . .
These are the very sinews of our Society; and whatever
weakens, or tends to weaken, our regard for these,
or our exactness in attending them, strikes at the very
root of our community.

—John Wesley[1]

In the eighteenth century, a small number of Anglican priests began preaching on the importance of justification (forgiveness, or pardon with God) by faith and the new birth (entering into a new relationship with God the Father as an adopted child). The best known of these priests were George Whitefield and John and Charles Wesley. Many of their contemporaries were more scandalized by the fact that they were preaching outdoors than by the content of their preaching. But these preachers, who soon became known as Methodists because of their methodical approach to the Christian life, were determined to preach to as many people as possible, and were willing to preach outside the walls of the church if it helped them reach more people.

Thousands of women and men were converted to the Christian faith by these Methodists. And, particularly through the efforts of George Whitefield, the message of justification by faith and new birth crossed the Atlantic Ocean, gaining momentum in the British colonies in America. The First Great Awakening was due largely to the traveling and preaching of George Whitefield throughout the colonies from 1739 to 1740. It was George Whitefield, then, and not John Wesley, who was largely the face of the eighteenth-century Evangelical Revival. By all accounts, Whitefield was the most dynamic preacher of his era. He traveled throughout England and the colonies in America, preaching to audiences that sometimes had tens of thousands of people. Whitefield was a better preacher than John Wesley. And in all likelihood his preaching resulted in the conversion to Christian faith of many more people than did John Wesley's. So why is it that today people often speak of the Wesleyan tradition, but never the Whitefieldian tradition?

One way of explaining Wesley's endurance as a key figure for contemporary Christians is his emphasis on small group formation, particularly the class meeting. It has frequently been noted that between Whitefield and John Wesley, Wesley was the more gifted organizer. A biography of Adam Clarke (who was a Methodist preacher during Wesley's lifetime) recounted Wesley's insistence that class meetings were essential to the revival:

From long experience I know the propriety of Mr. Wesley's advice: "Establish class-meetings and form societies wherever you preach and have attentive hearers; for, wherever we have preached without doing so, the word has been like seed by the way-side." It was by this means we have been enabled to establish permanent and holy Churches over the world. Mr. Wesley saw the necessity of this from the beginning. Mr. Whitefield, when he separated from Mr. Wesley, did not follow it. What was the consequence? The fruit of Mr. Whitefield's labor died with himself. Mr. Wesley's remains and multiplies.[2]

The author then recounted his memory of a conversation between George Whitefield and John Pool, as it was related to him by Pool.

Mr. P. was well known to Mr. Whitefield, who, having met him one day, accosted him in the following manner:

"*Whitefield*. Well, John, art thou still a Wesleyan?

"*Pool*. Yes, sir. I thank God I have the privilege of being in connection with Mr. Wesley, and one of his preachers.

"*W.* John, thou art in thy right place. My brother Wesley acted wisely; the souls that were awakened under his ministry he joined in class, and thus preserved the fruits of his labor. This I neglected, and my people are a rope of sand."[3]

According to Pool's memory, Whitefield himself conceded the value of the class meetings for the Methodist revival and wished he had been more proactive in maintaining them.

The most explosive growth of Methodism, however, actually came after the deaths of both George Whitefield and John Wesley. From 1776 to 1850 American Methodism grew like a weed. In 1776, Methodists accounted for 2.5 percent of religious adherents in the colonies, the second smallest of the major denominations of that time. By 1850, Methodists comprised 34.2 percent of religious adherents in the United States, which was 14 percent more than the next largest group![4] During this period, hundreds of thousands of people were coming to faith in Christ as a result of the preaching, testimony, and ministry of American Methodists. And throughout the period of this growth, every Methodist was expected to participate in a weekly class meeting.

A strong case can be made that the class meeting was the single most important factor to the growth of early Methodism and to the retention of converts within Methodism. People who had come to faith in Christ were immediately placed in a class meeting, where they would be helped to grow in their faith and where they would learn how to practice their faith.

So, how did class meetings come to play such a key role in early Methodism? And what happened in classes?

The Early Methodist Class Meeting: "Watching Over One Another in Love"

The class meeting was started in 1742 when a group of Methodists were trying to figure out how to pay off a building debt in Bristol, England. Captain Foy (who is otherwise unknown to historians) suggested that the Bristol society be divided up into groups of twelve people. One person in each group would be designated the leader and would be responsible for visiting everyone in the group every week in order to collect one penny from each of them. By this means, Foy believed the building debt could be retired. Someone raised a concern that this would prevent the poorest Methodists from being involved. Captain Foy responded by volunteering to take the eleven poorest members of the Bristol society into his group. He said that he would visit them each week and ask them if they could contribute. If they were unable, he would pay their pennies on their behalf. Then, he challenged the other people at the meeting to do the same thing.

As this plan was put into practice, it became apparent that many Methodists were not keeping the "General Rules," which every Methodist was expected to keep. The General Rules were: do no harm, do good, and attend upon the ordinances of God. While the first two are fairly straightforward, "attend upon the ordinances of God" referred to basic Christian practices or disciplines. Wesley explicitly mentioned public worship, ministry of the Word, the Lord's Supper, family and private prayer, searching the Scriptures, and fasting or abstinence.[5] Almost immediately, Wesley realized that the class leaders (the ones who had originally committed to make the weekly collection) were ideally situated to address the lack of discipline in keeping the General Rules among Methodists.

In the General Rules, Wesley described the duty of the class leader as follows:

> That it may the more easily be discerned whether they are indeed working out their own salvation, each Society is divided into smaller companies, called Classes, according to their respective places of abode. There are about twelve persons in every class, one of whom is styled *the Leader*. It is his business:
>
> > (1.) To see each person in his class once a week at least; in order

> To receive what they are willing to give toward the relief of the poor;
>
> To inquire how their souls prosper;
>
> To advise, reprove, comfort, or exhort, as occasion may require.

(2.) To meet the Minister and the stewards of the Society once a week, in order:

> To pay in to the stewards what they have received of their several classes in the week preceding;
>
> To show their account of what each person has contributed; and
>
> To inform the Minister of any that are sick, or of any that walk disorderly and will not be reproved.[6]

Initially, the class leader met each person at his or her own house. However, it was quickly decided that it would be more practical for the entire class to meet together once a week. Wesley reported that at the class meeting, "advice or reproof was given as need required, quarrels made up, misunderstandings removed. And after an hour or two spent in this labour of love, they concluded with prayer and thanksgiving."[7] Wesley further reported on what he believed were the fruits of the class meeting:

It can scarce be conceived what advantages have been reaped from this little prudential regulation. Many now happily experienced that Christian fellowship of which they had not so much as an idea before. They began to "bear one another's burdens," and "naturally" to "care for each other." As they had daily a more intimate acquaintance with, so they had a more endeared affection for each other.

And "speaking the truth in love, they grew up into Him in all things which is the head, even Christ; from whom the whole body, fitly joined together, and compacted by that which every joint supplied, according to the effectual working in the measure of every part, increased unto the edifying itself in love."[8]

The class meeting, then, quickly developed into much more than a capital campaign. It became a crucial tool for enabling Methodists to "watch over one another in love," to support and encourage one another in their lives with God. In fact, John Wesley thought the oversight and support that the class meeting provided was so important that it became a requirement for membership in a Methodist society. To be a Methodist meant that you were involved in a weekly class meeting.

So what happened in these weekly meetings?

Classes were intended to have between seven and twelve members in them. Women and men often, though not always, met together in the same class. The groups were also led by both women and men. Classes were divided primarily by geographical location. In other words, you would have attended a class meeting with the Methodists in your neighborhood. As far as the content or organization of the weekly meetings, the class meeting seems to have focused on three things. First, it held people accountable to keeping the General Rules. Second, the class meeting was a place where Methodists were encouraged to give weekly to the relief of the poor. Third, and most central to the time spent in the weekly meeting, it was a place where every Methodist answered the question, "How is it with your soul?" (Methodist historian Scott Kisker has recently rephrased this question as "How is your life with God?")[9]

Did you notice what did not happen in the early Methodist class meeting? These groups were not Bible studies. People did not study a book in these meetings. Among the purposes or goals of the class meeting, Wesley did not list the transfer of information from a perceived expert to a largely passive and ignorant audience. In other words, the class meeting was a very different kind of small group than the typical Sunday school class. Rather than being focused on transferring information or ideas about Christianity, the early Methodist class meeting was focused on helping people come to know Jesus Christ and learn how to give every part of their lives to loving and serving Christ.

The phrase that best captures what the Methodists believed was so important about the class meeting was "watching over one another in love." Early Methodists were asked to invite others into their lives and to be willing to enter deeply into the lives of other people so that together they would grow in grace. They were committed to the idea that the Christian life is a journey of growth in grace, or sanctification. And they believed that they needed one another in order to persevere on this journey.

And so, in the early Methodist class meeting, people would gather together, someone would open the meeting with prayer, the group would often sing a song or two, and then the class leader would start by answering the question, "How does your soul prosper?" After participants answered the question, the leader would turn to someone else in the group and ask that individual the same question. The class leader or someone else might occasionally respond to the person's answer by asking another question, offering encouragement, and sometimes giving advice. The basic pattern of the meeting was that simple. People were essentially giving testimony to their experience of God over the past week. And God seems to have used this, as the testimony of others was frequently contagious. People often experienced conversion simply through participating in a class meeting![10]

Wesley felt that the class meeting was so important that he believed that its decline would weaken Methodism itself. He wrote, "Never omit meeting your Class or Band; never absent yourself from any public meeting. These are the very sinews of our Society; and whatever weakens, or tends to weaken, our regard for these, or our exactness in attending them, strikes at the very root of our community."[11] The class meeting was one of two forms of small groups that held Methodism together, just as sinews connect muscle to bone, making it possible for arms and legs to move and function. In case this strong image was overlooked, Wesley continued by saying that if the class meeting was threatened, then the "very root" of Methodism itself was in danger.

The Pillars of Early Methodism

Much more could be said about the emphases of John Wesley and early Methodists. The key point for now is that the class meeting was the primary structure in early Methodism that was designed to keep every person connected to the rest of the movement, to make sure that people were doing all that they could to cooperate with the grace that God had given them and to ensure that no one was forgotten or left behind.

As Methodism was transplanted from British to American soil in the second half of the eighteenth century, the class meeting quickly became firmly rooted in the American context. One of the first appearances of Methodism in America was when a woman urged a family member to start a class meeting among friends and family who were falling away from the Christian faith after migrating to America from Britain. When Methodism became a formal denomination in 1784, the class meeting was listed as a requirement for membership. As a result, from its beginnings as a church in America, Methodists were committed to gathering together with a small group of Christians every single week to talk about their lives as followers of Jesus Christ, to check in and ask one another if they were growing closer to Christ or falling farther away. Attendance at a weekly class meeting continued to be a formal requirement in the Methodist Episcopal Church throughout its first decades. This was the most basic requirement of membership. It is what gave Methodist membership its meaning.

The expectation that members would participate in a weekly class meeting was formally spelled out in the first *Doctrines and Discipline of the Methodist Episcopal Church*. For example, the *1798 Doctrines and Discipline* stated the consequence of failing to attend one's class meeting as follows:

> What shall we do with those members of society, who wilfully [*sic*] and repeatedly neglect to meet their class?
>
> *Answ.* 1. Let the elder, deacon, or one of the preachers, visit them, whenever it is practicable, and explain to them the consequence if they continue to neglect, viz. Exclusion.
>
> 2. If they do not amend, let him who has the charge of the circuit exclude them in the society; shewing that they are laid aside for a breach of our rules of discipline and not for immoral conduct.[12]

In other words, American Methodists believed that this practice was so essential to what it meant to be a Methodist that they were willing to remove someone from membership if the person did not attend the class meeting consistently. For a period of time, Methodists even issued class meeting tickets to people each quarter that were used to gain admittance into the larger worship service. These tickets gradually became more of a symbol of Methodist identity and of the importance of the class meeting, without being used as a means of entry into the worship service. You can still find many class meeting tickets from the eighteenth and nineteenth centuries.

In the *1798 Doctrines and Discipline*, Coke and Asbury commented on their sense of the significance of the class meeting for Methodism. What follows is a lengthy quotation, but it reveals so much about *why* the early Methodists were committed to this practice that it is worth reading carefully.

> It is *the thing itself, christian fellowship* and not the name, which we contend for. The experience of about sixty-years has fully convinced us of its necessity; and we ourselves can say that in the course of an extensive acquaintance with men and things, and the church of God, for about twenty or thirty years we have rarely met with one who has been much devoted to God, and at the same time not united in close christian fellowship to some religious society or other [meaning a small group like the class meeting] . . .
>
> We have no doubt, but meetings of christian brethren for the exposition of scripture-texts, may be attended with their advantages. But the most profitable exercise of any is a free inquiry into the state of the heart. We therefore confine these meetings to *christian experience*, only adjoining singing and prayer in the introduction and conclusion. And we praise the Lord, they have been made

a blessing to scores of thousands . . . In short, we can truly say, that through the grace of God our classes form the pillars of our work, and, as we have before observed, are in a considerable degree our universities for the ministry.[13]

I am confident that Francis Asbury (who was essentially the John Wesley of American Methodism) would not mind if we changed the name of these groups. But I am also convinced that he would see the reclaiming of this practice as essential and urgent. Asbury testified that from his experience he rarely met a deeply committed Christian who was not involved in something like the class meeting. The fact that today so many Methodists are attempting to follow Christ in isolation reveals a serious disconnect from the riches of the Wesleyan heritage.

Read the second paragraph from the previous quotation from Asbury again. He concedes the value of Bible studies and other information-driven small groups. However, he insists that "the most profitable exercise of any is a free inquiry into the state of the heart." He then clearly states that the class meeting was limited to a focus on "Christian experience" and not on instruction in the content of the Bible or another study. The class meeting, according to Asbury, was the "pillar" of American Methodism's exponential growth as a movement in the late eighteenth and early nineteenth centuries. It was also the main way that new leaders were raised up and prepared for ministry within Methodism! We used to have an apprenticeship model to train people for ministry: you learned by watching someone else; then you did it with your mentor's guidance and supervision, and then you did it on your own. We now have a very different model, and it does not seem to be bearing fruit for the kingdom of God. During the period that the class meeting was a basic requirement of membership, the Methodist Episcopal Church grew from a few thousand members to 2.5 million.[14] But as Methodism began to distance itself from the class meeting, its growth also began to decrease, then stop, and finally decline.[15]

It is time for Methodists to become people of Wesley's method again.

Guide for Small Group Discussion

Organization:

:00–:15 Informal Conversation

Open with a Prayer

:15–1:00 Questions for Discussion

1. What were your general thoughts or reactions to this chapter? Was anything particularly exciting or challenging to you? Why?

2. This chapter suggests that one reason people who came to faith in Jesus through Methodist preaching persevered in their faith was because they were organized into small groups. How could your church do a better job of helping people grow and mature in their faith?

3. Were you previously familiar with the class meeting and its history in Methodism? Why do you think the class meeting was so important to early Methodist growth and discipleship?

4. What obstacles do you see that might make it difficult for your church to return to a practice like the early Methodist class meeting? How could these obstacles be most effectively addressed?

1:00–1:15 Transformation Question

Describe a time when you felt closer to God as a result of your participation in a small group. Or, describe a time when your faith was strengthened through an interaction with another person (perhaps through conversations, prayer, or Bible study with a pastor, mentor, or friend).

Close with a Prayer

3

Moving into God's House: The Theological Foundation of the Class Meeting

It is thus we wait for entire sanctification, for a full salvation from all our sins . . . It is love excluding sin; love filling the heart, taking up the whole capacity of the soul.

—John Wesley, "The Scripture Way of Salvation"[1]

As important as the class meeting was to spiritual vitality and growth in Wesleyan Methodism, the deep purpose of Methodism was not to get people into class meetings; rather, it was to help them come to faith in Christ and grow in that faith. In other words, the class meeting was essential to early Methodists *because* it was a logical practice based on their understanding of God. Wesley's preaching, essays, journals, and personal correspondence are filled with repeated and clear affirmations of the key doctrines of historic Christianity. When Wesley took steps to formally start a new denomination in America in 1784 (the Methodist Episcopal Church), he not only ordained preachers to lead the new church, but he also included Articles of Religion, which were concise statements of essential Christian doctrines, as well as a compilation of his own sermons, which most clearly expressed key Methodist beliefs. Wesley believed that vital Christianity was impossible without both right thinking and right acting. Thus, the "method" that gave Methodism its name arose out of a desire to practice the beliefs that John Wesley and others were preaching.

Yet, it is also important to be clear that for Wesley, orthodoxy, though essential to real Christianity, is not sufficient unto itself. Wesley's deep concern was with a lived faith, not only a mental assent to propositional truth. Right doctrine, or right beliefs, was important to Wesley because it provided necessary guides and boundaries for right living. In other words, orthodoxy (right belief) leads to orthopraxy (right practice). As we will see, holy living was the goal of the Christian life for Wesley, but he felt that you could not know what holy living looked like without sound Christian doctrine.

Toward the end of his life, in an essay on the future of Methodism, John Wesley wrote about his deep conviction that Methodism would have a bright future as long as it held fast to both Methodist doctrine, or teaching about God, and Methodist practice, or the "method" that gave the movement its name. Wesley wrote: "I am not afraid that the people called Methodists should ever cease to exist either in Europe or America. But I am afraid lest they should exist as a dead sect, having the form of religion without the power. And this undoubtedly will be the case unless they hold fast both the doctrine, spirit, and discipline with which they first set out."[2]

The majority of this book is focused on reclaiming the most basic part of early Methodist "discipline"—the class meeting. But Wesley prophesied in 1786 that Methodism would exist as a God-breathed movement only if it clung to the *doctrine, spirit, and discipline* that it started with. Wesley did not say that Methodism would have spiritual vitality as long as it held on to one of these, but that all three were important. In order to fully grasp the "Why?" of the class meeting itself, it is crucial to understand the key beliefs that informed the class meeting, which Methodists hoped to live out in their daily lives. My goal here is not merely to return to old ways; rather, I am convinced that Methodism will be renewed by the Holy Spirit when it clearly proclaims the gospel in its fullness and joins people together to support one another as they seek to faithfully follow Jesus Christ.

So what were the key doctrines or beliefs of the first Methodists? In 1746, John Wesley gave a fairly concise statement of the "main doctrines" of Methodists, "Our main doctrines, which include all the rest, are three, that of repentance, of faith, and of holiness. The first of these we account, as it were, the porch of religion; the next, the door; the third is religion itself."[3] Methodists preached about the possibility and urgency of moving not just a part, but *all* of our lives into God's house.

The Porch: Repenting of Sin

The starting point for John Wesley was that people are in desperate need of salvation and that we cannot save ourselves. In fact, the basic requirement for joining early Methodism was "a desire to flee from the wrath to come, to be saved from their sins."[4] In our context, one of the great challenges American Christianity faces is that salvation seems unnecessary to many Americans, who feel that they are the source of their own life and security. But the gospel is only good news to those who realize their need for salvation and that only God is able to save us. The good news is that God is able *and* willing to save!

Simply put, we are addicted to sin. Try as hard as we might, we return to sin repeatedly. We struggle to break destructive cycles, but too often return to them even when we know they are damaging to us and to others. While this is expressed in different ways for different people, the consequences are the same—sin has power over us. It is in control and we are not.

Sin affects us from the spectacular to the mundane. Examples of people committing spectacular and devastating sins abound in the news. Too often, it feels as though the local news is little more than a chronicle of the most devastating sins people have committed in the community. Thanks be to God, few people commit egregious sins, such as murder. But can anyone say that they are entirely without greed, envy, anger, sloth, lust, gluttony, or pride? Do we never gossip, talk bad about others, or withhold praise from those who deserve it? The list could go on. Rather than loving God and others, too often we are obsessed with ourselves. Sin is felt not only in personal relationships, but also in broader social ways. The sin of racism in the United States, for example, not only impacted African-Americans prior to the civil rights movement, it continues to have an impact on both the structures of American society and on interpersonal relationships. Social sin is all the more devastating because when individuals bump up against it, they often feel powerless to change it.

John Wesley discussed the human tendency to pursue the things of this world instead of the things of God: "What is more natural to us than to seek happiness in the creature instead of the Creator? To seek that satisfaction in the works of his hands which can be found in God only? What more natural than the desire of the flesh? That is, of the pleasure of sense in every kind?"[5] In another sermon, "The One Thing Needful," Wesley further argued that there is nothing more important for people to do than to turn from sin and seek the salvation that only God can bring:

> To recover our first estate, from which we are thus fallen, is the one thing now needful—to re-exchange the image of Satan for the image of God, bondage for freedom, sickness for health. Our one great business is to rase out of our souls the likeness of our destroyer, and to be born again, to be formed anew after the likeness of our Creator. It is our one concern to shake off this servile yoke and to regain our native freedom; to throw off every chain, every passion and desire that does not suit an angelical nature. The one work we have to do is to return from the gates of death to perfect soundness; to have our diseases cured, our wounds healed, and our uncleanness done away.[6]

As a result, for Wesley "original sin," or the idea that we are in a mess that we cannot get ourselves out of, was not an optional belief for Christians. Wesley asked, "Is man by nature filled with all manner of evil? Is he void of all good? Is he wholly fallen? Is his soul totally corrupted? Or, to come back to the text, is 'every imagination of the thoughts of his heart evil continually'? Allow this, and you are so far a Christian. Deny it, and you are but an heathen still."[7] In the previous passage, Wesley cited Genesis 6:5, which reads, "The LORD saw that the wickedness of humankind was great in the earth, and that every inclination of the thoughts of their hearts was only evil continually" (NRSV).

This can all sound pretty discouraging. But for Wesley, this was simply the reality of the situation in which we find ourselves. Wesley was convinced that there *is* good news! However, we cannot fully recognize how *good* the news is until we recognize how deeply we need it. God knows where we are but is not content to leave us there. For Wesley, God wants "to renew our hearts in the image of God, to repair that total loss of righteousness and true holiness which we sustained by the sin of our first parent."[8] We are able to experience all that God wants for us after we recognize the situation we are in and that we do not have the resources to save ourselves. The first step, then, is to "repent, that is, know yourselves . . . Know thyself to be a sinner."[9] Repentance involves a recognition of the reality of the grip of sin on one's life *and* a decision to turn away from sin and turn toward God. Repentance, then, is not only having your eyes opened to reality; it involves a 180-degree turn, so that one turns completely away from sin and turns toward the new life offered in Jesus Christ.

Wesley was convinced that the Christian life cannot make sense apart from the conviction that all people need to be saved, that we are not capable of saving ourselves, and that Jesus is not only able to save us but is ready and willing to do for us and in us what we cannot do on our own. Methodist practice, then, was based on a sober assessment of humanity's situation combined with a deep and abiding hope in the work that God has already done in Christ in order to make it possible for us to be restored to God's presence. Repentance is essential because it brings us to the porch of God's house, where we recognize our need for God and begin to seek God's amazing grace.

Faith: Entering into Salvation in Christ

Once we have recognized the reality of our situation before God and have decided to turn away from the sin in our lives, having stepped onto the porch of God's house, what comes next?

After we recognize our need for salvation and our complete inability to be the source of our salvation, we can turn away from ourselves and turn to Christ in faith (and even this is only possible by God's grace). We can recognize the reality that God has already done everything in Christ that needs to be done in order for us to be forgiven of our sins and reconciled to God. The theological term for the forgiveness of sins that comes through Jesus Christ is *justification*. Here is how Wesley described it:

> The plain scriptural notion of justification is pardon, the forgiveness of sins. It is that act of God the Father whereby, for the sake of the propitiation made by the blood of his Son, he "showeth forth his righteousness (or mercy) by the remission of the sins that are past" . . . To him that is justified or forgiven God "will not impute sin" to his condemnation. He will not condemn him on that account either in this world or in that which is to come. His sins, all his past sins, in thought, word, and deed, "are covered," are blotted out; shall not be remembered or mentioned against him, any more than if they had not been. God will not inflict on that sinner what he deserved to suffer, because

the Son of his love hath suffered for him. And from the time we are "accepted through the Beloved," "reconciled to God through his blood," he loves and blesses and watches over us for good, even as if we had never sinned.[10]

In other words, because of Christ's righteousness, and the sheer gratuity of God the Father, the righteousness of Christ is applied to us, resulting in the pardon, or forgiveness, of all our past sins. *All* of our past is washed, or covered in Christ. It is "blotted out," meaning that it is no longer held against us or remembered by God. God loves, blesses, and watches over us as if we had lived a life of complete righteousness before God, just as Jesus himself did.

Did you catch the full significance of this?

First, when we recognize the reality of sin, that we have wronged as well as been wronged, and then turn to Christ, we are fully forgiven. Second, when we turn to Christ, we are not just forgiven, but we are ushered into a new relationship with God the Father, a relationship where we are adopted as God's own children!

So how does this happen? For Wesley it is freely given; we seek it only by faith. So, what is faith? According to Wesley, faith in Christ

is not barely a speculative, rational thing, a cold, lifeless assent, a train of ideas in the head; but also a disposition of the heart . . . It acknowledges the necessity and merit of his death, and the power of his resurrection. It acknowledges his death as the only sufficient means of redeeming man from death eternal, and his resurrection as the restoration of us all to life and immortality . . . It is a sure confidence which a man hath in God, that through the merits of Christ *his* sins are forgiven, and *he* reconciled to the favour of God; and in consequence hereof a closing with him and cleaving to him as our "wisdom, righteousness, sanctification, and redemption" or, in one word, our salvation.[11]

Faith is personal; it is something that must be intimately connected to your own life and experience. It is not something that can be inherited or passively handed down from one generation to the next. As has often been said, "God does not have grandkids." The news that is even better, though, is that faith does not need to be—indeed, should not be—tentative. It is a "sure confidence" of one's complete forgiveness and reconciliation to God—everything isn't just okay; it is fantastic!

New Birth: Crossing the Threshold of God's House

Justification is by faith, and it is essentially the experience of being forgiven of your past sins. But this experience is so profound that it also leads to transformation. Forgiveness leads to a fresh start, one that is so all-encompassing that it is properly seen as a "new birth." Wesley described justification as "that great work which God does *for us*, in forgiving our sins."[12] And he described the new birth as "the great work which God does *in us*, in renewing our fallen nature."[13] In another sermon, Wesley compared justification and the new birth as follows:

> Though it be allowed that justification and the new birth are in point of time inseparable from each other . . . justification implies only a relative, the new birth a real, change.

God in justifying us does something *for* us: in begetting us again he does the work *in* us. The former changes our outward relation to God, so that of enemies we become children; by the latter our inmost souls are changed, so that of sinners we become saints. The one restores us to the favour, the other to the image of God. The one is the taking away the guilt, the other the taking away the power, of sin.[14]

One way of thinking about this would be to focus on Wesley's description of the shift from being an enemy of God to becoming a child of God. At one level this can be seen as a relative change, a change of status. But at another level, becoming a child of God cannot leave one unchanged. Being embraced as God's beloved child is itself transformative.

Too often, the Christian life is drastically abbreviated, where the entire goal is to be justified by faith in Christ. In this view, justification by faith is like crossing the finish line. The goal is to experience salvation by faith, and forgiveness is the end of the race. Wesley reminds us that the image of new birth is also found in Scripture and cannot be abandoned. One of the best examples is in John 3:3–7:

Jesus answered, "I assure you, unless someone is born anew, it's not possible to see God's kingdom." Nicodemus asked, "How is it possible for an adult to be born? It's impossible to enter the mother's womb for a second time and be born, isn't it?" Jesus answered, "I assure you, unless someone is born of water and the Spirit, it's not possible to enter God's kingdom. Whatever is born of the flesh is flesh, and whatever is born of the Spirit is spirit. Don't be surprised that I said to you, 'You must be born anew.'"

When the full witness of Scripture is included, the image shifts considerably. Instead of seeing justification by faith as the end, it morphs into the starting line. Now that your past has been fully addressed, forgiven, and redeemed by God in Christ, you are given a fresh start, sin no longer reigns, and you are able to live a new life of faithfulness. Note, then, that being forgiven of past sins and entering into God's household is not the end; it is only the beginning!

A reasonable question at this stage would be, "Can I know that I have been forgiven and born again?" This question is important because there have tended to be two extremes when thinking about the new birth. On the one hand, the need for new birth is sometimes downplayed because someone was raised a Christian. On the other hand, Christians have sometimes talked about being born again in ways that can make it seem forced, or contrived. Scripture provides the solution to either extreme. In Romans 8:14–16 Paul described the inner witness of the Holy Spirit that testifies to us that we are God's children: "All who are led by God's Spirit are God's sons and daughters. You didn't receive a spirit of slavery to lead you back again into fear, but you received a Spirit that shows you are adopted as his children. With this Spirit, we cry, 'Abba, Father.' The same Spirit agrees with our spirit, that we are God's children." Wesley often pointed to what wonderful news this promise is, describing it as "an inward impression on the soul, whereby the Spirit of God directly 'witnesses to my spirit that I am a child of God'; that Jesus Christ hath loved me, and given himself for me; that all my sins are blotted out, and I, even I, am reconciled to God."[15]

In other words, whether someone has been a Christian for as long as they can remember, or they are attending a revival service and are wondering whether they should respond to the altar call, Wesley says, based on Romans 8, that you can know whether you are a child of God because a privilege of all of God's children is that the Holy Spirit witnesses to them of their adoption. God is so gracious that not only are we offered undeserved forgiveness of our sins and the opportunity to start anew, but also the Spirit testifies inwardly to us of God's love for us after we have faith in Christ. In the words of Charles Wesley's hymn "O For a Thousand Tongues to Sing," after the new birth, "you then shall know, shall feel your sins forgiven."[16]

Growth in Holiness: Moving All of Your Life into God's House

If repentance is the porch of God's house, and faith is the door, the new birth is when you cross the threshold of God's house, and holiness is the process of moving our lives completely into God's house. In one of his best-known sermons, John Wesley put it this way, "At the same time that we are justified, yea, in that very moment, *sanctification* begins."[17] Just as *justification* is the theological term that refers to pardon, or the forgiveness of our sins, *sanctification* is the theological term that refers to holiness, or becoming Christlike. And *both* justification and sanctification are by faith. Wesley was adamant that holiness is by God's grace and comes through our faith in God: "We are sanctified, as well as justified, by faith . . . Faith is the condition, and the only condition of sanctification, exactly as it is of justification."[18]

And here is where Wesley's vision for the possibility and potential of the Christian life really takes off:

From the time of our being "born again" the gradual work of sanctification takes place. We are enabled "by the Spirit" to "mortify the deeds of the body," of our evil nature. And as we are more and more dead to sin, we are more and more alive to God. We go on from grace to grace, while we are careful to "abstain from all appearance of evil," and are "zealous of good works," "as we have opportunity doing good to all men"; while we walk in all his ordinances blameless, therein worshipping him in spirit and in truth; while we take up our cross and deny ourselves every pleasure that does not lead us to God.

It is thus that we wait for our entire sanctification, for *a full salvation from all sins*, from pride, sell-will [*sic*], anger, unbelief, or, as the Apostle expresses it, "Go on to perfection." But what is perfection? . . . Here it means perfect love. It is *love excluding sin*; love filling the heart, taking up the whole capacity of the soul.[19]

This is a powerful vision for the Christian life! And it is one that Wesley insisted on until the end of his life. Wesley was adamant that whether it is called "entire sanctification," "perfect love," or "love excluding sin," God wants to free us from all that pulls us away from living fully in Christ. He also insisted that this complete freedom from sin is by grace through faith. In fact, he often reminded his audience that if they were seeking it by faith, and not by works, there was nothing they had to do themselves before they could be entirely sanctified. This meant that they should hope for and expect "perfect love" now. Wesley wrote, "If you seek it by faith, you may expect it *as you are*: and if as you are, then expect it *now*."[20] Wesley was so committed to the doctrine of entire sanctification that in the last decade of his life he wrote that entire sanctification was the "grand depositum" of Methodism and was the reason that God had brought Methodism to life.[21]

I have been surprised and disappointed by how much resistance there is to John Wesley's emphasis on the extent that we can become holy, by the grace of God, *in this life*. Wesley believed that by God's grace we could be made perfect in love in this life. By "perfect," Wesley meant love excluding sin. When I was in seminary, one of my professors put it this way: Christian perfection, or entire sanctification, means giving all that I know of myself to all that I know of God. This is a dynamic process because tomorrow I will know more about myself than I do today, and as a result, I will have more of myself that I can give to God. I will also continue to learn more about myself over time, so there will be more that I can give to the God I am coming to know more and more.

The idea of perfection does not get great press in popular society. Now that I listen for it, I am amazed at how often I hear people say things like, "Nobody's perfect." Initially, I was surprised to hear people say this to dismiss the seriousness of the moral failing of an athlete, for example. But I have been even more disheartened with how often I have heard church leaders say something along these lines in order to essentially excuse sin, or a lack of faithfulness to the gospel, in advance. At one level, I understand. If you were to ask me for empirical evidence of people messing up or making mistakes, I could rattle off countless examples. And more important, we are not perfect as we are, and we do not make ourselves perfect.

But here is the irony: Many people also struggle to affirm the doctrine of original sin (the idea that every person has been deeply damaged by the consequences of sin) and, as a result, that sin is inevitable and unavoidable, making it necessary for us to be saved by the grace of God. Yet, the same people who deny original sin, who feel that people are not *that* bad, are also adamant that nobody is perfect, that no one is capable of living a life free of willful sin. So, which is it? Are we capable of avoiding sin, or *in*capable of avoiding sin? The operating view of too many people is something like, "People aren't all that bad, but they are also incapable of being all that good." What a depressing (and inaccurate) view of human nature and the possibility of life in Christ!

Here is why I believe in Christian perfection: I believe that it is possible for people to give themselves completely to God, perfectly, because I am convinced that grace is bigger and more powerful than sin. Now, don't mistake me. I believe that sin is real and devastating in its effects. But I do not believe that it is necessary. And whether intentionally or not, if you deny the possibility of living an entirely faithful life, then you are arguing that sin is necessary in some sense and that it *must* exist in this world, even if God hates it.

I am certain that holiness is a real possibility *in this life* because Jesus Christ has been raised from the dead. Sin and death have done all that they could; they have shown themselves completely in all their terror and destructiveness. On Good Friday, when Jesus' dead body hung limp on the cross, it looked as though sin and death had won, that they could not be vanquished from this world. That life would always be accompanied by sin. But on Easter Sunday, the tomb was empty! Sin and death could not contain the life that was in Christ. Jesus conquered sin in its most terrifying and ultimate expression—death. Jesus overcame even death itself. And so, we can proclaim with Paul, "Where is your victory, Death? Where is your sting, Death?" (1 Cor. 15:55). Jesus gives us the victory. Jesus has shown us that God does not make pacts or compromises with sin. The resurrection shows us that sin is no longer necessary. It may remain in our lives and in the lives of others, but it no longer reigns. In the power of Christ and his resurrection, those who experience new life in Christ can be completely freed from sin's hold on their lives. Holiness is not about what you can do for God, it is about the possibilities for faithfulness and living in God's will that have been broken open by the explosion of grace that has been made available to us through the work of Christ. We should settle for no less than the fullness of the salvation that has been offered to us in Christ in this life and the life to come.

For Wesley, the purpose of Methodism was "to spread scriptural holiness."[22] Wesley was convinced that the Bible teaches that we can not only find forgiveness for past sins, but that we can find new life in Christ and go on to perfection. We can experience deep healing of all that separates us from the love of God in Christ Jesus. And so, "May God himself, the God of peace, sanctify you through and through. May your whole spirit, soul and body be kept blameless at the coming of our Lord Jesus Christ. The one who calls you is faithful, and he will do it" (1 Thess. 5:23–24 TNIV).

But Wesley's experience with the Methodist movement convinced him that people rarely made progress in moving their lives into God's house by themselves. Wesley insisted on the necessity of the class meeting, then, because he believed that God used this form of small group practice to help people continue pursuing Christ and growing in their love of God and neighbor. In fact, Wesley explicitly criticized George Whitefield's inattention to the class meeting in Pembrokeshire in his published *Journal* in 1763:

> I was more convinced than ever that the preaching like an apostle, without joining together those that are awakened and training them up in the ways of God, is only begetting children for the murderer. How much preaching has there been for these twenty years all over Pembrokeshire! But no *regular societies*, no discipline, no order or connection. And the consequence is that nine in ten of the once awakened are now faster asleep than ever.[23]

We would not have to try all that hard to make connections from what Wesley found in the 1760s in Pembrokeshire to contemporary Wesleyan and Methodist faith communities.

It is time for Methodists to return to the doctrine, spirit, and discipline with which we first set out.

Guide for Small Group Discussion

Leaders: Note that the time for discussion is decreased by five minutes this week and five minutes is added to the discussion of the Transformation Question.

Organization:

:00–:15 Informal Conversation

Open with a Prayer

:15–:55 Questions for Discussion

1. What were your general thoughts or reactions to this chapter? Was anything particularly exciting or challenging to you? Why?
2. Which of these beliefs do you find easiest to affirm or most central to being a Christian?
3. What ideas, if any, from this chapter were the most difficult for you to follow or agree with? Why?
4. Do you agree with Wesley's understanding of Christian perfection? Are there legitimate reasons that holiness, or deep obedience to Christ, is impossible? If so, why?

:55–1:15 Transformation Question

Can you tell a story of when you (or someone you have observed) stepped onto the porch of God's house, crossed the threshold into God's house, or moved your life more completely into God's house?

Close with a Prayer

4

Becoming Wesleyan Again

We have no doubt, but meetings of christian brethren
for the exposition of scripture-texts, may be attended
with their advantages. But the most profitable exercise
of any is a free inquiry into the state of the heart . . .
Through the grace of God our classes form the pillars
of our work, and, as we have before observed, are in a
considerable degree our universities for the ministry.

—Francis Asbury and Thomas Coke,
1798 Doctrines and Discipline[1]

Acommon method (joining every Methodist to a class meeting) and a common message (the necessity of repentance, faith, and holiness) were at the center of Methodism during its periods of most explosive growth. If the class meeting was central to early Methodist vitality, why was it eventually abandoned? A brief glimpse at the decline of the class meeting may help us have a better understanding of where we are currently and how we can reclaim the practice that helped so many people grow in their faith in Christ.

The Death of the Class Meeting

The decline of the class meeting began in the mid-nineteenth century. The move away from the class meeting could be discussed in a variety of ways. One explanation is that the rise of the Sunday school movement gradually pushed the class meeting to the margins of Methodism, ultimately causing it to disappear altogether. Another explanation, perhaps not unrelated to the first, is that as Methodists became increasingly affluent and upwardly mobile (as Methodism moved from being a predominantly lower-class movement toward becoming a middle- and upper-middle-class denomination by the end of the nineteenth century), they were less and less comfortable talking to each other about the details of their lives as followers of Jesus Christ. The results of upward mobility and the Sunday school movement led to an approach to small groups where a group of people gathered to learn from a perceived expert, either the leader of the small group or the author of a book the group was studying. In other words, the Sunday school movement shifted attention away from the focus on Christian experience and on becoming a deeply committed Christian, which Asbury had so strongly endorsed.

To be fair, Sunday school has had a positive impact on many people's lives. As I was working on this book, a friend who is an exceptional pastor told me that Sunday school was a key context for him where he first began to experience leadership in the church, leading to his sense of being called to ordained ministry. And my guess is that many people who are reading this book have also had a positive experience with Sunday school. You may remember reading a book that really helped you think about things in a different way, or you may have been in a class that was led by a gifted leader who touched your life because she cared about you so much. If you have had this experience, then you have a better sense of what a class meeting is all about than you may realize. Class leaders checked in on the people in their classes throughout the week to see how they were doing, trying to encourage them in their faith. Ultimately, I suspect that most of the examples that people would cite of Sunday schools that were transformative for them would have more to do with the quality of the leader and a personal connection to someone in the group than to curriculum or content.

Here is one example of why I think that small groups like the class meeting are more effective tools for Christian discipleship than Sunday school: I recently participated in a Sunday school class that read a book that argued that Christian discipleship should include a deep concern for global poverty. The study was very well conceived, organized, and presented. The leader was well prepared and organized each week. There was a video clip we watched that was professional, high quality, and engaging. We even had lively discussions about the problem of poverty and what we as Christians were called to do about it, both individually and as a church. Based on my experience, it would be difficult for a Sunday school class to be better thought out or executed.

As far as I could tell, every single person who attended the study of the book was challenged and convinced by the argument. And yet, there was no indication that anyone's life actually changed as a result of the study. To be blunt, I think what ultimately happened is that we felt guilty about the gap between the material comfort we experience as Americans and what people lack in other parts of the world. This feeling of discomfort lasted throughout the study, and some people probably thought very seriously about doing something. However, there was no clear call for the group to make a commitment and there was no opportunity that I recall for individuals to share what they were going to do as a result of the new information they had received in the study.

I think people did gain new ideas through the study. But I am afraid they probably did not experience the transformation that Jesus wants them to experience as his followers.

To return to the decline of the class meeting, then, as people increasingly participated in Sunday school, they had less time for other things. And as people committed to a weekly Sunday school class, being involved in a weekly class meeting seemed less important and even redundant. In part, the class meeting seemed less important because people were not making the case for the need for "Christian experience" as aggressively as they had been. Interestingly, the place where class meetings tend to be seen the latest in American Methodism is in new Methodist communities. Local histories of Methodism, particularly in places that mark the church's westward expansion, typically cite class meetings being formed as part of Methodism's initial presence. The class meeting seems to have been a part of Methodism's DNA as a movement, so that even as the class meeting was rapidly declining on the East Coast, it was still being used in new faith communities as the church expanded toward the West Coast. And when B. T.

Roberts, who would become the key leader of the Free Methodist Church, was expelled from the Methodist Episcopal Church in 1858, he was particularly concerned about restoring the class meeting and a clear emphasis on proclaiming the doctrine of entire sanctification.[2]

Where Methodism has been marked by the renewing presence of the Holy Spirit, people have typically met in classes. Decline seemed to be, at least in part, connected to an abandonment of the class meeting, just as Wesley predicted. When people meet together and talk about their pursuit of God, and their experience of God, the Holy Spirit seems to show up and draw people closer to Christ. Even as this decline was occurring, there were some who lamented the demise of the class meeting. Peter Cartwright, a nineteenth-century Methodist preacher, for example, wrote this about his sense of the importance of the class meeting and his concern about its demise:

> Class-meetings have been owned and blessed of God in the Methodist Episcopal Church, and from more than fifty years' experience, I doubt whether any one means of grace has proved as successful in building up the Methodist Church as this blessed privilege . . . In these class-meetings the weak have been made strong; the bowed down have been raised up; the tempted have found delivering grace; the doubting mind has had all its doubts and fears removed, and the whole class have found that this was "none other than the house of God, and the gate of heaven." Here the hard heart has been tendered, the cold heart warmed with holy fire; here the dark mind, beclouded with trial and temptation, has had every cloud rolled away, and the sun of righteousness has risen with resplendent glory, "with

healing in his wings"; and in these class-meetings many seekers of religion have found them the spiritual birth-place of their souls into the heavenly family, and their dead souls made alive to God . . .

But how sadly are these class-meetings neglected in the Methodist Episcopal Church. Are there not thousands of our members who habitually neglect to attend them, and is it any wonder that so many of our members grow cold and careless in religion, and finally backslide? Is it not for the want of enforcing our rules on class-meetings that their usefulness is destroyed? Are there not a great many wordly-minded [sic], proud, fashionable members of our Church, who merely have the name of Methodist, that are constantly crying out and pleading that attendance on class-meetings should not be a test of membership in the Church? . . . Just as sure as our preachers neglect their duty in enforcing the rules on class-meetings on our leaders and members, just so sure the power of religion will be lost in the Methodist Episcopal Church.

O for faithful, holy preachers, and faithful, holy class-leaders! Then we shall have faithful, holy members. May the time never come when class-meetings shall be laid aside in the Methodist Episcopal Church, or when these class-meetings, or an attendance on them, shall cease to be a test of membership among us. I beg and beseech class-leaders to be punctual in attending their classes, and if any of their members stay away from any cause, hunt them up, find out the cause of their absence, pray with them and urge them to the all-important duty of regularly attending class-meeting. Much, very much, depends on faithful and religious class-leaders; and how will the unfaithful class-leader stand in the judgment of the great day, when by his neglect many of his members will have backslidden, and will be finally lost?[3]

Unfortunately, by the beginning of the twentieth century, the class meeting was almost entirely extinct in America. It was occasionally referred to by historians, but it was far easier to find an early Methodist class meeting ticket than a group of Methodists who were actually meeting together as a class meeting. Instead of talking to each other about their experience of God and their pursuit of holiness, Methodists were talking to each other about much more general and abstract ideas that were increasingly difficult to connect to the intimate and mundane details of their lives. The class meeting had become an archaeological relic of our better days and instead of being a way of life, people began to view their Christian identity as one of a number of hobbies they might develop or work on when it was either convenient or served to make life a little bit better.

Why We Should Return to This Practice: The Value of the Class Meeting for the Twenty-First Century

The decline of the class meeting matters because disciples of Jesus Christ are called to live different lives, not just think different thoughts. Here is a way of thinking about what is at stake: A year from now, would you rather know more *about* the kind of life you want to live, or have made progress in *living* that kind of life?

If your goal is to be a disciple of Jesus Christ and most of your focus has been on finding the church that will best meet your needs, figuring out which translation of the Bible is the best, or reading the best books on discipleship that you can find, but your life is the same as it was before—I would argue that you aren't becoming a disciple. Nothing other than following Jesus Christ can make you his disciple.

Here's another way of illustrating what I'm trying to get at: Imagine a person who sets a goal to run a marathon. They might spend time researching the best kind of running shoes to wear, the best shorts, the best approach to training, and the healthiest food to eat. They might subscribe to *Runner's World* and even read it. But no matter what else they do, there is one thing that is absolutely essential to being able to run a marathon—running. A person can research and buy all the gear that they want, but if they don't actually start running, they are not making real progress toward completing a marathon. It is that simple.

I am worried that our approach to Christian discipleship is too often like a person who prepares to run a marathon by buying shoes without actually running in them. Please don't misunderstand me; just as good running shoes are essential for long-distance running, the Bible and the church are essential for discipleship. Discipleship, however, is about a way of life, not only the life of the mind. Disciples *follow* Jesus. They are *sent out* in ministry by Jesus. They *heal* the sick. They *feed* the poor. They *tell* people about Jesus and what he has done.

I am convinced that a recovery of the class meeting would be used by God to help people who are interested in Christian discipleship to make real and meaningful progress toward becoming deeply committed followers of Jesus Christ.

Another reason I am so excited by the possibilities of a recovery of the class meeting is because returning to this practice would do more than improve the quality of discipleship of those who are already committed Christians. One of the most important contributions the class meeting can make to contemporary Christianity is that it provides an entry point for every Christian to be in connection with a small group of people in a way that is focused on the dynamic process of the Christian life. In general, the Christian life is a fluid process. People tend to either grow and mature in their faith or decrease in their commitment to their faith. The class meeting is a helpful tool for increasing the likelihood that people will move forward in their faith for at least two key reasons:

1. *The class meeting joins people together in small groups so they are not lost in church.* While this may seem most common or most likely in large churches, people can be "lost" in even the smallest churches. In churches of any size, there are people who are connected with the church in some way, but who are not really known by other people in the church. Though this is almost always unintentional, when a church does not plan for ways to try to connect every person who is involved in the life of the church, someone is inevitably going to be left on the sidelines. The class meeting provides a structure that can connect everyone to a small group of people within the community of faith. And even more important than whether people are connected is whether they are in a relationship with Jesus Christ and are growing in that relationship. The focus of the class meeting on each member's experience of God provides a helpful weekly reorientation for each person and for the entire church that this is the most basic and most important thing that a church should do—help its

members enter into a relationship with the living God and grow in that relationship.

2. *The format of the class meeting draws attention every week to the reality that the Christian life is not static.* Related to what has just been said, in a class meeting each participant is reminded every single week of the importance of living their beliefs. Answering the question, "How is it with your soul?" Or, "How is your life in God?" every week helps to keep "the main thing the main thing." In the class meetings of which I have been a part, simply knowing that I will answer that question each week helped me to become more aware of how God was at work in my life and how I was cooperating with God's grace, or failing to cooperate with God's grace. The content of the class meeting, then, is the lives of the people who are present. The goal of the class meeting is the growth in holiness of the members of the class, helping each person grow in their love and knowledge of God and in their love of others. Regardless of where someone finds themselves spiritually, they can recognize the truth of their current relationship with God, and then seek to move forward.

Participating in a class meeting does not guarantee that you will become a mature Christian. It is not a magic bullet that is guaranteed to make you a saint. But participating in a class meeting will create space in your life for you to give voice to your victories and struggles. This discipline will result in your being more aware of what is going on in your own relationship with God. It will also help you know what is happening with other people in your faith community. One of the major benefits of this is that you will be better able to pray for others and they will be able to pray for you with increased specificity.

An Entry Point

Another reason why Methodists should return to a small group like the class meeting is because of its potential to be a valuable point of entry for people who are not Christians or for people who are nominal Christians (people who are Christian in name only, but not really practicing their faith). There may have been a time when the church could expect people to come to them. In the 1950s in the United States, for example, being a good American was sometimes seen as synonymous with being a Christian. God and country were often deeply intertwined in popular consciousness. This is less and less the case today. In fact, because of the vast size and population of the United States, Christians in other countries are increasingly coming to see the United States as a country needing to be evangelized and are sending missionaries to the U.S.

People are less comfortable visiting churches than they may have been several decades ago. Though it may be hard for people who have gone to church their entire lives to understand, folks who are genuinely "unchurched" may not feel comfortable visiting a church. They may not realize that they are welcome to show up at any time without being invited (in part because we seem to invite people to church less and less frequently). They also may not be sure what clothes to wear, or they may be concerned that things will happen in the worship service that won't make sense, or that they won't know how to respond. There are a number of obstacles that make visiting a church intimidating even to those who might be interested.

The advantage of the class meeting is that people do not have to attend church in order to attend a class meeting. I would certainly hope they would eventually choose to become involved in the life of the church. But which do you think would be least intimidating to a guest: going to a large building you have never been to before and figuring out how to park and where to go (all this after you have researched where the church is, what time the services are, etc.); or going to someone's house to attend a smaller gathering of five to eleven other people, at least one of whom you already know because they invited you? My sense is that most people would find it quite a bit easier to start by meeting with a few other people in someone's home. And as a very practical matter, when they do decide to go to a worship service, they will already know the members of their group when they get there.

The class meeting, then, has strong potential to help Christians to become more faithful disciples of Jesus Christ *and* to be a valuable tool for evangelism. The class meeting could provide a way to invite new people into the community of faith and into a saving and life-changing relationship with Jesus. During the '50s and '60s, large revivals were often used to introduce thousands of people to the Christian faith. Billy Graham was the best known of these traveling evangelists. During his crusades, Graham would travel across the country, preaching for several days in a particular location. This was an effective approach to evangelism in the '50s and '60s (though too many who made commitments at Billy Graham Crusades never became a part of the life of a local church). But we no longer live in the '50s and '60s.

In our current context, the class meeting provides a structure that is ideal for inviting new people to encounter and enter into a relationship with Jesus. The smaller size of the class meeting and its location in one of the group members' homes make it more hospitable to visitors. In addition, truly unchurched people don't have a strong sense of what to expect when they begin to engage the ministries of the church. As a result, some of the things that might seem a bit odd to you about having someone's first experience with church be a class meeting would not seem weird to them at all. If unchurched people were invited to join class meetings, it could become a place of conversion, just as it was in early Methodism!

Simply put, class meetings are designed for anyone who wants to grow closer to God. They can help ensure that people don't fall through the cracks in a church. They can also help people be more aware of what is going on in their own lives as Christians, reminding them that being a Christian should make a meaningful difference in their lives. And class meetings provide a place for people to talk to others who want to grow closer to God about what is happening in their life with God, even if they would not yet consider themselves to be Christian and they just want to explore salvation in Christ.

Though the class meeting is, at best, an endangered species in Methodism, it is *already* being reclaimed by several faith communities that are seeking to return to early Methodism's vision for raising up Christians that are not Christian in name only, but in convictions and in the way they live their lives. In the early 1990s, Christ United Methodist Church in Ft. Lauderdale, Florida, experienced deep renewal, in large part because of their recovery of class meetings, which they called "Wesley Fellowship

Groups." Here is the testimony of Beverly Payne, a member of Christ Church, to the impact that these groups had on the church:

> In Wesley Fellowship Groups, we were encouraged to share our lives, hold each other accountable, pray together, study scripture, and commit ourselves to outreach. We were also made aware that to share our experience with others, we would need to "parent" and "grandparent" new groups to fulfill our commitment. [One of the ways they did this was by encouraging groups to leave an empty chair in the room, as a reminder that the group was always open to new members.]
>
> Out of these close-knit groups, individuals began to feel and know that God had a specific plan for their lives. Persons began to experience God's call to lead and do things far beyond their felt capabilities.[4]

We have also already read the testimony of Nick Weatherford, a member of Munger Place Church, about the impact the class meeting (they call the groups "Kitchen Groups") has had on his own life and on the culture of the congregation. Munger Place is a powerful example of the way Methodism can be resurrected through a return to its Wesleyan roots. Munger Place was initially founded in 1913 and was a vibrant congregation for decades in the heart of east Dallas. However, the congregation began to decline toward the end of the twentieth century. By 2009 the congregation was no longer financially viable, likely having ceased to be spiritually viable several years before. The church was closed for over a year and was resurrected in October 2010. A major part of this resurrection was campus pastor Andrew Forrest's commitment to reclaiming the equivalent of the class meeting. As of this writing, the church has established seventeen class meetings, and they have actually struggled to train leaders fast enough to start new groups for all the people who are interested in joining them!

As I began talking about writing this book and my passion for reclaiming the class meeting, I have been amazed at how many pastors, lay leaders, and local churches are interested in returning to this practice (many are already doing so). People want to be in relationship with other Christians! And they want their faith to make a difference in the way they live their lives. That is what class meetings are supposed to do, and so far none of the substitutes for the class meeting have done a better job of helping Christians "watch over one another in love" and encourage each other to grow in their love for God and neighbor.

Many churches in the Wesleyan/Methodist tradition are dying because they have abandoned one of the greatest insights of their heritage: disciples are not made through study; they are formed through an apprenticeship. This book has come out of a lingering conviction that there is nothing that we can do that would be more certain to bring renewal to Christianity than a recovery of the early Methodist class meeting, and the beliefs that informed this practice.

A Concern: Is This Judgmental and Exclusive?

One of the most common objections I hear to returning to the class meeting comes from the concern people have that any form of "accountability" will lead to being judged or excluded. Many people are afraid that if others really knew them, they would not be accepted or loved. The concern is, *If I don't meet your expectations, will you exclude me? Will you tell me that I am not good enough?* So, is the class meeting judgmental and exclusive?

At one level, the class meeting appears to be a place where judgments are made. And it is a place of exclusion (because some people are in the group, but not everyone can be in it and the group still function as it is intended to function). But before you reject the class meeting, please hear me out. First, unlike the early Methodist class meeting, I am not advocating that people who do not regularly attend class meetings should be expelled from church membership. And my deep desire is to include as many people as possible in these groups! Second, in early Methodism there were actually two kinds of transformation-driven small groups: the class meeting and the band meeting. The band meeting was even smaller than the class meeting, it was voluntary, and it was specifically for people who had already crossed the threshold of faith in Christ and could speak of an experience of new birth. The focus of the band meeting was weekly confession of sin. Much more could be said about the band meeting (it may be that you will find this to be a practice worth reclaiming as well); however, since this book is focused on the class meeting, the important thing to note is that the class meeting was not as in-depth and intense a form of accountability as the band meeting.

So, in general, the class meeting should not really be a place where judgments about your life are being made. And it would be very rare for someone to be asked not to return to the group. At the same time, it seems to me that our concern to avoid being judgmental or exclusive is often overdone, especially because I'm not convinced that these can be avoided entirely or that they are inherently bad. We make judgments about things all the time, and often without thinking about it, we include some things and exclude others. As one example, the decisions we make about how we spend our time mean that we are deciding to do one thing, which inevitably excludes all the other possible ways we could spend our time at that moment. Avoiding judgment and exclusion altogether is impossible and undesirable. Instead, the concern should be focused on what judgments are being made and what is being excluded. In contemporary Methodism, one of the quickest ways to dismiss something is to label it as judgmental or exclusive. But could it be that there is a place for both in the church and in the Christian life?

Again, what we are excluding makes all the difference. Let's look at exclusion more carefully. The first Methodists were obsessed with trying to figure out how best to exclude sin from people's lives. They were clear that there are things that are not of God, that keep us from growing in our relationship with God. If we are to pursue growth in holiness, these things must be excluded. They are not neutral. It is not a matter of indifference if they are allowed to reign in our lives.

I doubt many people would argue that Christians should not try to remove sin from their lives. What may be more controversial is that early Methodists also excluded people who were not serious about following Christ. The Methodist movement was not designed to make people comfortable in listless, apathetic discipleship. Rather, it was designed to help people experience the fullness of the abundant life that God offers every single person in Christ.

Hear me carefully: I believe that contemporary Methodism should welcome every single person, should reach out to every single person with the good news of what God has done for them in Jesus Christ. A key Wesleyan belief is that the gospel is not only for some; it is for everyone. *All may be saved.* In that sense the message of contemporary Methodism should be radically inclusive. But contemporary Methodism should not pass out cheap grace. We should not tell people it is okay if they profess faith in Christ but do not allow it to impact the way they live their lives. Put differently, the consequences of sin are devastatingly serious and cannot be ignored. God's desire is to exclude sin from our lives.

In order to be a faithful follower of Jesus Christ, sin must be judged and removed from one's life. The very definition of Christian perfection, which was the goal of the Christian life for John Wesley, was "love excluding sin."[5] Related to this, Methodists may need to take another look at whether it is a good idea to unreflectively reject the possibility of excluding people who are not interested in following Christ. Ultimately, I would not advocate literally excluding people from the UMC, but I would recommend that the church cease catering to people who are interested in the church only because it makes them feel comfortable, because it is their country club. The efforts and energies of the church should be focused on proclaiming the good news and inviting people into new life in Christ.

There are two particular things I want to say about the concern to avoid being judgmental in an attempt to reclaim the class meeting for the twenty-first century. First, the fear of being judged seems to be related to a deeper issue—trust. Imagine having lunch with a perfect stranger, someone you have never met. How would you feel if they began to express concerns about the way you were living your life? I know I would not feel good about such unsolicited feedback from a stranger.

Now imagine having lunch with the person you trust and respect more than anyone else in the world. How would your reaction be different if they expressed similar concerns? I hope your reaction would be very different. There are a handful of people in my life to whom, if they sat me down and expressed concerns about decisions I was making, I would listen very carefully. There are people I trust and respect so much that my instinct would be that they could see things about my life more clearly than I can. I would listen and likely take their advice because I know they love me. I know they care about me more than about whatever part of my life we are discussing.

Having said that, I don't think the contemporary class meeting is best thought of as a place where other people make judgments about your life. In the classes of which I have been a member, it has been rare for someone to judge me or call me to account for something.

This leads to the second point about judgment: the primary person judging you in a class meeting should be yourself. The class meeting is a place where you take a weekly inventory of your own life. You make judgments about how things are going in your life with God. Some weeks you will judge that things are going quite well and that you have been particularly aware of God's grace and have cooperated with this grace. Other weeks, you will judge that things are not going very well. On other occasions, you may be doing everything right, and yet, God seems strangely distant. The point is that in a class meeting, it is not the group's job to tell you about your relationship with God. Rather, you are telling the group about your experience from the past week. The members of the class meeting should support you and pray for and with you as you seek to grow as a follower of Christ.

Successful class meetings will be places where members are able to speak into each other's lives in ways that are life-giving. Sometimes someone may speak a word of encouragement that is particularly helpful in a specific situation. And members will exhort one another to continue to pursue Christ, whether they are already in a living relationship with Jesus, or are just beginning to seek him.

One More Thing: Don't Let the Name Be a Distraction!

Finally, the name "class meeting" is unfortunate because what we are seeking to reclaim is essentially the opposite of a "class." The word "class" had a very different connotation in early Methodism than it does for us today. What we call these small groups that are focused on lives transformed by the grace of God is ultimately not important. In most contexts, in fact, it should probably be replaced with something else. I am not arguing for reclaiming a set of ideas about discipleship. I am praying that Christians will gather together in small groups to talk about their discipleship, how they are experiencing God's transforming presence in their lives, and how it is changing their lives. I am praying that through committing to talk about our lives in God, people will experience an assurance of God's love for them that will breathe new life into their relationships with God.

I have spent a lot of time (probably far too much!) trying to come up with the perfect new name for twenty-first-century class meetings. At this point, the ideal name for twenty-first-century class meetings has eluded me. I can think of several possibilities that would be good for one reason or another. However, I have not been able to come up with the perfect name that would fit every conceivable context where class meetings might thrive. I am confident that the Holy Spirit will guide you to the best name for your particular context. I am also certain that the name isn't as important as the practice. In order to emphasize the continuity with the vitality of early Methodism, I will continue to refer to these groups as class meetings throughout this book.

We have previously discussed Munger Place Church's reclaiming the class meeting. They call their groups Kitchen Groups. LifeChurch.tv, a nondenominational church started by former Methodist pastor Craig Groeschel, has a small group ministry that bears remarkable similarity to the early Methodist class meeting. They call their groups Life Groups. The retrieval of this practice by Christ United Methodist Church in Florida led to significant spiritual and numerical growth within the church. They called their groups Wesley Fellowship Groups. All of these names are great for different reasons. I've also thought of Transformation Groups (to highlight the emphasis on being transformed), Discipleship Groups (to emphasize that the goal is becoming a disciple of Jesus Christ), and Centering Groups (to focus on the way these groups help members center their lives in Christ). Use one of them if it is helpful to you, or come up with a better name and tell me about it! Ultimately, the name is not important; watching over one another in love is.

Guide for Small Group Discussion

Organization:

:00–:15 Informal Conversation

Open with a Prayer

:15–:55 Questions for Discussion

1. What were your general thoughts or reactions to this chapter? Was anything particularly exciting or challenging to you? Why?

2. What has your experience with Sunday school or other informational approaches to the Christian life been like? Do you resonate with the example from the chapter of the study that argued that Christians ought to be concerned for the reality of global poverty? Why or why not?

3. What do you think about the author's argument for the potential contribution that a return to the class meeting could make for Christianity today? Were there parts with which you particularly agreed? Parts with which you disagreed? Are there ways that small groups that already exist in your church could become more effective, in the ways that have been discussed in this chapter?

4. Do you have concerns about feeling judged or excluded if you were to participate in something like a class meeting? Why or why not? Do you think there are ways those concerns could be addressed,

or that the problem you are identifying could be mitigated?

:55–1:15 Transformation Question

Thinking back to the differences between planning to run a marathon and actually starting to run, would you say your efforts to follow Jesus are more like someone who is actively training, or more like the person who is reading a lot of magazines and buying running gear, but not actually running yet? Why?

Close with a Prayer

5

The Basics: From Start to Finish

> Within six months of beginning our first twenty
> Wesley Fellowship Groups, I began to sense that
> God was doing a new thing at Christ Church.
> There was a movement of the Holy Spirit.[1]
>
> —Dick Wills, *Waking to God's Dream*

Though you have already read quite a bit about the class meeting, much of what has preceded this chapter has been focused on *what* a class meeting is and on making the case for *why* we should return to the class meeting. The rest of the book discusses *how* to actually start class meetings. This chapter describes how to start class meetings from the ground up. The next chapter outlines the crucial role of the class leader to a successful group and the ways a class leader can be most likely to succeed. Chapter 7 identifies some of the obstacles to the vitality of a small group, and discusses how to overcome them. And the final chapter points to the keys to a life-changing class meeting.

Great Expectations

My assumption is that most people who read this book will be involved in a church where implementing this approach to small groups will require a change in the culture of the congregation (or at least a part of the culture of the congregation). I would love to see a major shift in the Wesleyan/Methodist family from information-driven small groups to a transformational approach to small groups. I have spoken with many pastors and lay leaders who have a similar desire to see a cultural shift occur, where the expectations in a congregation move from an acceptance of nominal Christianity that is not doing a whole lot of work in most people's lives to expecting God's grace to be manifest in amazing and life-altering ways.

I am also reminded of the wise counsel a friend of mine gave me not too long ago: Don't let perfect be the enemy of good. On the one hand, I want people to have "great expectations" for what can happen in their churches—because with God all things are possible! On the other hand, we should not be demoralized because the entire approach of a church does not change overnight.

The best way to move forward is to control what you can control. If you are a pastor, you can preach and teach about the truth that God's grace not only pursues us and forgives us, but it also heals us and makes us new. You can also commit to participate in such a group and actively recruit other people to participate in these groups, and lead them. If you are a layperson, you can start a group, lead a group, or simply be a faithful participant in one. You can also commit to ask others to join a group with you.

The expectations of membership in most Methodist churches, and really most congregations in the United States in general, have been so low for so long that many people who are members of a church may simply not be willing to join a group that requires weekly attendance and a willingness to talk about the ways they are experiencing (or not experiencing) God's grace in their lives. You cannot control the level at which someone else is willing to commit to their faith. You *can* decide to invest more deeply in your own faith and invite others to join you.

Any step toward greater faithfulness is cause for rejoicing! If you can get one group like this started in your church, but it is the only one, you should celebrate that a group of people have committed to "watch over one another in love" who would otherwise have been more isolated in their faith. Something is better than nothing!

And Yet, a Cultural Shift Is Possible!

One of the major success stories of the retrieval of class meetings by a contemporary church was Christ Church, a Methodist church in Fort Lauderdale, Florida. The church experienced deep renewal in the 1990s, largely because "Wesley Fellowship Groups" became a part of the culture of the congregation. Dick Wills, who was the senior pastor at the time and subsequently became a bishop in The United Methodist Church, described the role of these groups in the renewal of his congregation in his book *Waking to God's Dream*. Wills became so convinced of the importance of these groups, which were modeled after the class meeting, that he believed "that being in a small group is as important as being in worship each week." Here is his testimony of the impact of committing to these groups at his church: "Within six months of beginning our first twenty Wesley Fellowship Groups, I began to sense that God was doing a new thing at Christ Church. There was a movement of the Holy Spirit. As the leader, I now knew the direction in which God was leading our congregation. The most exciting days for Christ Church were just ahead of us."[2]

In a recent conversation with Bishop Wills, he indicated that these groups were most likely to succeed when the senior pastor championed the groups publicly and consistently before the entire congregation. This also meant that the senior pastor needed to be in a group, not merely advocating their benefit with no real connection to one. In other words, the leader of the congregation must be willing to go where he or she leads.

At Christ Church, there was a significant shift in the culture of the congregation as a result of the move to Wesley Fellowship Groups. By the time Wills left the church to serve as a bishop, the church had 170 of these groups! And the church began to function more as a church *of* small groups, rather than a church *with* small groups. In other words, the key place where people felt connected to the church was through the deep relationships they formed in their "Wesley Fellowship Groups." Another key way that Wills lifted up the value of these groups was by regularly having people who had experienced life change through their involvement in these groups testify to their transformation during worship.

Christ Church, under the leadership of Dick Wills, provides a concrete example that the culture of a congregation can be changed by the grace of God. The story of this church also offers another testimony that class meetings continue to be an effective means by which people experience God's transforming grace.

Starting Somewhere

In places where a group like the class meeting will be almost entirely novel, the best way to start would be for the senior pastor to introduce the entire congregation to the class meeting by preaching a sermon series on the key theological emphases of the Wesleyan/Methodist tradition, with particular focus on the "method" of small groups that focused on growing in faith and were essential to bringing this message to life.

At the end of the sermon series, the pastor could then ask people to pray about whether God is calling them to lead or join a group like this. I would also recommend that the pastor approach women and men directly that already evidence gifts for leading a group like this. And if a pastor is committed to helping members become disciples, then the most gifted spiritual leaders in the church should be asked to lead a class meeting before they are asked to do anything else. This position should be seen as the most important role in the church, if the church is to accomplish its mission of helping people become disciples of Jesus Christ. This mission is far more likely to be accomplished by class leaders than by the chairs of the finance committee, staff parish relations, church council, or the trustees. It is not that these positions are unimportant, but that people have limited time and energy to give, and the most gifted and spiritually mature in the church should be asked to lead a class meeting before they are asked to do anything else. (Some folks may be willing to be involved in more than one way, and someone who is gifted to be the chair of the finance committee may not have the gifts to be a class leader, and vice versa.)

Once a group of class leaders has been identified, there should be a brief training session (approximately three hours). This book could be used to provide a foundation for the training, particularly chapters 5–7. The key topics to cover during the training would be:

- The role and function of the leader (facilitator, not teacher)
- The dynamics of small groups (dealing graciously with people who talk too much, have all the answers, struggle to share at all, etc.)
- Anticipating the development of the group itself (life cycle of small groups)
- Examples of groups that are functioning well and groups that are not functioning well
- Where to go and who to contact with questions or for help

In my conversation with Bishop Wills, he indicated that a key to the success of the Wesley Fellowship Groups at Christ Church was that the groups were recruited by the leader. While I do not think this is essential (Munger Place has assigned the groups, and this has also generally worked well), there are several advantages to the leader recruiting their own group. When the class leader draws together people to form a group, the group will more likely already have some degree of chemistry, because at a minimum the members will be connected to the person who starts the group (as opposed to, for example, simply having people sign up for groups based on the time that is the most convenient for them to meet). Another advantage is that the leader will tend to be more invested in the group, because they have been given ownership of the group from the outset. It is crucial to the success of class meetings that the class leader is given both the responsibility and the authority they need in order to thrive.

One significant drawback is that the groups will be much likelier to be homogenous; i.e., the leader will likely tend to recruit people who look like him or her, which can significantly undercut the potential for learning to grow not only in your love of God, but in your love of neighbor. This could be addressed in the leader training, where the leaders could be encouraged to try to include people from different backgrounds and age groups. Christ Church worked to ensure a culture of hospitality in the groups by always leaving one chair empty as a reminder that new people were always welcome and that the group should be actively seeking to fill the empty seat.

It may be easier to assign people to groups in a new church start that is making the class meeting a part of the core of who it is as a church (like Munger Place). And in an established church (like Christ Church) that has not had these kinds of groups, it may be helpful to have a leader who takes responsibility and initiative in gathering a group together. However the groups are formed, the process should be bathed in prayer. The people forming the groups should ask the Holy Spirit to guide them. They should also consider inviting people who are inside and outside of the church, as the class meeting could be a more comfortable way for someone to begin to be involved in a local church than by attending a larger worship service, which can be a more overwhelming and difficult place to meet people.

After the class leaders have been trained and the prospective members have been identified, the potential members should be asked if they would be willing to join the group. Before approaching people, the class leader should be prepared to explain succinctly and clearly what a class meeting is (and remember it is more than fine to call it something entirely different from "class meeting") and why they are passionate about starting one. In other words, if you are starting a class meeting, you should be ready to define and explain the basics of the group to someone who knows nothing about it. The main thing you should be sure to communicate is that the group is designed to provide a place for people who want to know God, or know more of God, to grow—starting where they are. It is also a good idea to emphasize that this is not a study or a Sunday school class. Depending on the level of familiarity people have with this kind of group, it may help people take the step of trying a class meeting if the group initially meets for a limited amount of time.

This book itself is intended to be a resource to help class leaders get started. It can be used as an eight-week introduction that will help the group transition from an information-driven small group to a class meeting. The length of this study can also provide a natural time for assessing whether the group wants to continue to meet. Wills noted in Christ Church's use of Wesley Fellowship Groups that they ask all new members of the church to commit to explore small groups by being in a Wesley Fellowship Group for six weeks. The church found that "98 percent of the people who try a Wesley Fellowship Group for six weeks will stay."[3] Not a bad rate of retention in helping new members continue to grow in their commitment to their faith!

Laying the Foundation

One of the best ways to approach the challenges that can come with leading a small group is to get ahead of conflict by being proactive in setting expectations. If the class leader gently reminds the group from time to time that everyone in the group will lose out if all are not able to talk about their experience of God over the past week, then people will be more likely to police themselves. It is also helpful to acknowledge that some people process by talking and that those people tend to talk more than others. These folks may need to think more carefully about what they are going to say ahead of time to be sure that they don't unintentionally monopolize the group.

As the group begins to become more comfortable with being more vulnerable with each other, and as they talk directly about the state of their souls and their present relationship with God, it is important to acknowledge that this can be uncomfortable to some people. For those who have not previously spent much time talking with others about their relationship with God, it can be intimidating to try to say anything at all about their relationship with God. People should be encouraged that answering the question becomes more natural in time, and more important, that people will find that they begin to interpret their lives through the lens of their faith and, as a result, find that they are experiencing God in newer and deeper ways than they have before.

The Life Cycle of a Group

Small groups inevitably grow, change, and go through phases of development. Awareness by the group of these stages can help change that is normal be productive and positive rather than draining. Though every group is unique and has its own identity, small groups typically go through the following stages in their development: *birth*, *establishing a routine*, *questioning and refining purpose*, and *maturity*.[4]

1. Birth

In the beginning, or birth stage, of a group, the group begins to meet and is fairly dependent on the leader for direction and guidance. People sometimes feel a bit awkward or uncomfortable as they are getting to know one another and are increasing in their comfort with other members of the group. In this stage the leader plays a very visible role in providing structure and direction for the group. The leader is the primary person who casts the vision for what the group is about and what it is intended to do in the lives of the members. The leader also eases the initial discomfort that some may feel about what they are supposed to be doing by being the first one to discuss the state of his or her soul and by guiding the conversation from one person to the next.

2. Establishing a Routine

As the group transitions, people will become more comfortable with the basic rhythm of the group, and members will feel increasingly comfortable with each other. The key to establishing a routine is simply time and meeting regularly for several weeks.

One of the goals of this book is to help ease the transition through the first two stages by providing helpful guidance, direction, and purpose to the group. It is also intended to help the members gradually adjust to talking about their relationships with God more than they may have been used to. As a result, the "Guide for Small Group Discussion" adapts to the length of time that the group has been meeting, allowing for more time for discussing the content of the study in the beginning and less time for the Transformation Question. By the end of the study, there is less time focused on the content of the study and more time focused on the Transformation Question. The goal is to ease the group into the ideal format for a class meeting over the initial eight weeks that the group is meeting, with the hope that the group will continue meeting as a class after the study has been completed.

3. Questioning and Refining the Purpose of the Group

After the group gains some stability and direction, groups will often go through a period of questioning their purpose. I can still remember my initial experience with this phase the first time I started one of these groups. The group had just come to a place where it felt as though we were comfortable with each other, and several people had recently expressed very positive feelings about the group and the way it was helping them to be much more aware of whether they were really focusing on their relationship with God and how they were living out their faith at work or at home. I was shocked, then, when just a few weeks later the mood of the group seemed to shift dramatically. Several members began asking some very basic questions that really caught me off guard, like: "Is this it?" "Is this all we are going to do?" "Is there going to be more?" and "When are we going to go deeper?"

I was unprepared for these questions about the basic purpose and rhythm of the group. Looking back, it would have been more effective if I had allowed for the questions to be asked to the entire group. I would have responded more effectively if I had understood that people were trying to figure out just how deep they were willing to go. In this stage, the best thing the group leader can do is to be honest about their hopes for the group, while also making room for others to share their thoughts as well.[5]

One of the most positive outcomes of the questioning-and-refining stage is a much stronger sense of ownership by the entire group. In the beginning stage and the routine stage, the leader plays a crucial role in leading the group and owning the purpose of the group on behalf of the entire group. In the questioning stage, the group collectively wrestles with its purpose and may redefine it or clarify it in a way that will allow the entire group to go deeper. This process is not necessarily explicit, and the leader should not force a conversation like this to occur. It is something that usually happens naturally. This is also when deeper patterns, sensibilities, and assumptions become fairly rooted in the group. It can also be an ideal time to start a new group.

4. Maturity

Finally, the group will enter the stage of maturity. At this stage, the group will either adapt and change based on the evolving needs of the group, or it will die. The leader can play a key role here in helping the group to navigate this process. Leaders and group members need not be anxious about this stage, because both outcomes can be healthy. Sometimes the best thing for a small group is for it to expire, so the members can be released to be a part of new groups. The group I was in at Munger Place died, but its death was certainly not a failure, as it resulted in five new groups.

Our group was very tight-knit and had an implicit, but very deep, sense of purpose. As a result of journeying together through the "Questioning and Refining Stage," we all knew what the group was about. One of the main goals of the group was to experience a class meeting in order to make a group like it a fundamental part of the DNA of this new church of which we were all a part. As a result, we knew we would need to be willing to give up our comfort in the group for the sake of multiplying these groups and making them available to as many people as possible. In our case, we ended up dividing our group of ten people into five groups with two leaders. We then added six to eight new people to each group. This meant that the group immediately grew from one group of ten people to five groups with about fifty total people! It was hard for all of us to give up the familiarity and comfort of the group we knew so well, but it was rewarding to see so many people enter into the same type of groups that had been such a blessing to us.

This will not be the right approach in all contexts. Another way to multiply the groups would be for the leader to identify someone they feel would be a great leader and "apprentice" that person. The apprenticeship would primarily consist of the potential leader being given increased responsibility within the group. This person would open the group in prayer, lead the group a few times, and receive prayers and feedback from the initial leader. After the apprentice has observed the leader and led the group a few times, he or she can then be sent out (with a prayer of blessing, of course!) to start a new group.

During maturity, the group may also continue to adapt to the changing dynamics of the group. There is no need to set an arbitrary time on how long these groups will last. Here, class meetings are similar to Sunday school classes—some last for decades, and some last for months.

A Key to a Successful Group: You

The most important ingredient to a successful group is you! Your honesty with your group is crucial to its success. Your prayers for your group and individual members will be an enormous asset to the group's endurance and growth. Your willingness to be vulnerable and share openly, as well as to make sure you don't monopolize the conversation, will make the experience more powerful for everyone else. It really isn't that hard. The main thing you need to do is be willing, by the grace of God, to grow in your love for God and other people—and to be willing to do so within the context of a supportive community of faith.

Guide for Small Group Discussion

Leader: Note that the time for discussion is decreased by an additional five minutes this week, and five minutes are added to the discussion of the Transformation Question.

Organization:

:00–:15 Informal Conversation

Open with a Prayer

:15–:50 Questions for Discussion

1. What were your general thoughts or reactions to this chapter? Was anything particularly exciting or challenging to you? Why?
2. What is your church's current approach to small groups? Do you think your church is generally open to moving toward something like a class meeting? Why or why not?
3. What did you think about the summary of the role of Wesley Fellowship Groups at Christ Church? Do you think your faith community is being led to something similar? Why or why not?
4. Did the summary of the life cycle of a small group make sense? Have you been in groups where you experienced the group go through one of the phases that was described? What was it like?

:50–1:15 Transformation Question

How do you presently feel about the value of committing to a weekly small group where you talk about your relationship with God with other people? Do you sense God saying anything to you about your participation in a group like this? If yes, what are you hearing?

Close with a Prayer

6

The Role of the Class Leader

The revival of the work of God does perhaps depend
as much upon the *whole body of leaders*, as it does
upon the *whole body of preachers*.

—Francis Asbury and Thomas Coke,
1798 Doctrines and Discipline[1]

In the last chapter, we discussed the basics of
starting a class meeting. This chapter focuses
on the role of the class leader for the most effective class meetings. If you are reading this book as a part of a small group, it may
seem odd to have a chapter about leading the group in week six
of eight total weeks. I chose to include this chapter as a part of
the regular book for a few reasons. First, some may use this book
as a study of the class meeting, in order to discern whether the
group is willing to start a class meeting. In other words, this book

may be used by groups that don't yet have a class leader. If this is the place your group is in, I hope this chapter will help you better understand the role of the class leader, as well as help you discern whether you are being called to lead the group when it transitions to a class meeting.

The second reason I am including this chapter here is because the entire group will be stronger if there is a common sense of what the leader's role is (and perhaps what it is not). If your group already has an identified class leader, and you are not it, you can think as you read about the ways you can be a better participant in the group. And finally, and most importantly, I wanted to include this chapter here because my hope is that this book will be used to start multiple class meetings. You may not be the leader of your group now, but God may lead you to take on the role described here in the future. If you are called to become a class leader, you will be more prepared to do so having read and discussed this material.

Reclaiming Lay Spiritual Leadership

In early Methodism, the class leader was a crucial position. They were seen as the spiritual leaders of the people in their class meetings. The leader kept track of attendance and visited people who missed the weekly meeting. They also provided support and encouragement as needed. I believe that this role and the ability of churches to identify gifted class leaders will be one of the most important factors in the success or failure of the class meeting in our contemporary context. Here is how the significance of the class leader was described by Francis Asbury in the *1798 Doctrines and Discipline*:

The office is of vast consequence. The revival of the work of God does perhaps depend as much upon *the whole body of leaders*, as it does *upon the whole body of preachers*. We have almost constantly observed, that when a leader is dull or careless or inactive—when he has not abilities or zeal sufficient to reprove with courage though with gentleness, and to press a present salvation upon the hearts of the sincere, the class is, in general, languid: but, on the contrary, when the leader is much alive to God and faithful in his office, the class is also, in general, lively and spiritual.[2]

Today, many people point to the lack of lay leadership as a key and particularly disheartening sign of decline in the church. Some have sought to raise up a new generation of class leaders through a variety of approaches.[3] If the goal is to retrieve something like the class meeting, the best way to prepare people to become class leaders may be to simply introduce them to the class meeting itself.

In early Methodism, there was no separate training for being a class leader. A class leader's preparation was his or her prior experience of being in a class meeting and observing the class leader. The difficulty today is that there are very few functioning class meetings. So, class leaders cannot initially be trained by being in a class meeting, as they will often be starting class meetings from scratch. The goal of this chapter, then, is to provide an introduction to the function of a class leader and practical steps for becoming one. Before we go further, it is important to keep in mind that the key to being an effective class leader is *primarily* being in a living relationship with Jesus and being willing to talk to others about that relationship and encourage them to talk about their relationship with God.

Recognizing and Helping Alleviate Fears

In an online conversation about the contribution that reclaiming the class meeting could make for contemporary Methodism, someone raised an important concern: "Didn't the class leader have a role that included giving advice and/or reproof as needed? It seems like that would be felt as more intense to most people today . . . more intense than many folks want."[4]

As far as I can tell, this is a valid concern. There are at least two broad reasons that someone might resist joining something like a class meeting today. First, Methodists (in general) have not been in the habit of talking about their lives in God for a long time. Second, there is a strong desire in contemporary Methodism to avoid being judgmental or condemning, which has unintentionally resulted in a near-total abandonment of any real standards or expectations for membership. In most churches, to join the church you do have to make certain vows to be actively involved in the life of the church; however, few congregations hold their membership accountable for actually keeping these promises in any meaningful way. In current practice, there is no cost (financial or otherwise) associated with being a Methodist.

So, at one level people might be uncomfortable because they are being asked to talk about something they aren't used to talking about with other people. At another level they might be uncomfortable because they are being asked to make a meaningful commitment to join together with a small group of people with the purpose of growing in their lives with God.

Class leaders need to be aware of, and sensitive to, these concerns. One of the key things they should do in the beginning of the group is help participants be willing to recognize the importance of placing faithfulness to the gospel ahead of comfort. Comfort is not ultimately the best indication of whether something is good for you or you need to do something. Class leaders should acknowledge that talking to other people about your relationship with God may seem very risky, vulnerable, or scary. That is okay. It is normal and understandable. But choosing to follow Christ is worth the risk. Ultimately, I believe that there are many people who want to grow closer to God so much that they are willing to move outside of their comfort zone and take a risk if they are convinced that the risk is likely to help them actually grow in their faith. If you commit to leading a class meeting, you will be blessed to be a part of helping people experience the fullness of what God wants for their lives.

Thus, one of the main roles of the class leader is to help each member of the class meeting become more comfortable talking about the state of his or her soul. As a leader, among other things, you should help the class recognize that comfort is not necessarily the best indicator of right or wrong, or of what is best for us. Class leaders need to help people become more passionate about pursuing a personal relationship with Christ than about staying in their comfort zone.

Shepherding

One helpful image for thinking about the role of the class leader is that of a shepherd. The imagery of the class leader as shepherd is helpful for fleshing out the function of the class leader for the contemporary church. The class leader is the shepherd of his or her flock, and as such there are two key things that a class leader should do: (1) go after lost sheep; and (2) keep the rest of the sheep moving in the right direction. By "lost sheep," I mean someone who stops coming to the class meeting. When this happens, the class leader should be the first person to go after them, expressing that they have been missed, asking if they are doing okay, and also asking if they are willing to come back to the class meeting. This can be done a variety of ways. The most effective approach would be for the class leader to contact anyone who missed the previous meeting in a fairly informal way (a phone call would be ideal) immediately after the meeting. The basic message should be something simple and positive, such as, "I noticed you weren't at our meeting tonight and just wanted to touch base to see if you are doing okay and to ask if there is any particular way that I can be praying for you." This would also be a good time to state that you hope to see them at the next meeting. If the person misses the next week, the leader could ask if they would be available to meet for lunch or coffee. The goal here is to reestablish contact with the person and to express care for them. The leader should again ask the person how they are doing, express that they have been missed by the group, and indicate that the group hopes they will be able to return.

Note: If at any time someone clearly states that they are no longer interested in being a part of the class meeting, this decision should be accepted. Class leaders should never be like some telemarketers who refuse to take no for an answer and call repeatedly. The goal is not to harass people. And we should always respect people's decisions, even if we are grieved by them. Some might find this hard to accept, but this is in keeping with

God's own posture toward us. (See, for example, the story of the prodigal son in Luke 15:11–32.) The basic purpose of following up with folks who miss a meeting is simply to let them know they were missed. One of the reasons people often begin to distance themselves from a group is because they do not feel as if their presence is significant.

The class leader is also not the only person who could contact a member who was absent. Ideally, the members of a class meeting will come to care for one another to the extent that they will naturally be in touch with each other throughout the week, checking on one another and communicating support and prayers on behalf of one another. If you are not a class leader and you notice that someone was absent and you want to let them know they were missed, by all means give them a call!

The second way the class leader functions as a shepherd is that they keep the group moving in the right direction. The class leader is the one who is responsible for making sure everyone has a chance to answer the question, "How is your life in God?" They are also responsible for making sure that something else does not take over the class meeting. For example, the leader will ensure that the group does not become a curriculum-driven group, but continues to be a place where people watch over one another in love and discuss the current state of their souls. And most boldly, as the shepherd of the flock, the class leader, by the grace of God, seeks to move the class away from sin and closer and closer to mature discipleship.

One of the ways to help the class leader most effectively shepherd the conversation is to give the entire class meeting a basic introduction to small group dynamics. This will be discussed further in chapter 7, but for now the point is that one of the best ways to help class leaders shepherd a class meeting is to disarm some of the things that most commonly happen that derail the success of a small group. The responsibility for leading the meeting ultimately falls to the class leader. But if the group has already been made aware, for example, that some people process by talking and struggle to not dominate a conversation, it will be easier for the class leader to gently move the conversation forward if someone unintentionally does begin to dominate the conversation. Another added benefit is that group members who do tend to dominate the conversation may become more self-aware, recognizing their tendency to take over a conversation, which is itself a key first step toward discontinuing this bad habit.

Further, as the shepherd of a class meeting, the class leader is the one who should begin and end the meeting with a prayer (or ask someone else, in advance, if they would be willing to pray), and then the class leader should begin the meeting by being the first one to answer the question, "How is your life in God?" This is important because it gives an example of how the question can be answered for any new visitors and it eases the anxiety and uncertainty in the group about who is going to go first. After the leader is done, she should ask the next person the question.

There is one significant problem with the analogy of the class leader as shepherd: A shepherd is not a sheep! But a class leader *is* a member of the class meeting and *is* a fellow traveler on the way of discipleship. In other words, a class leader is *not* superior to the rest of the members of the class meeting. Rather, she is someone who may have more experience with being in a class meeting and the dynamics of the group and, as a result, is willing to offer herself as an example and a guide to the rest of the group.

In my mind, the most significant aspect of the class leader's role as the shepherd of the group is that they provide a model for the rest of the group. As a new class meeting begins, many of the people in the group will be uncertain of how to answer the basic question, "How is your life in God?" Some will struggle to go very deep at all. Without someone in the group providing an example to follow, people in the group may fall into the habit of stopping short of answering the question. Instead, they may give a summary of the highs and lows of the past week, not necessarily connecting the good things and bad things that happened to their Christian walk. Others lack a sense of appropriate boundaries in an entry-level group like this. They may be tempted to immediately jump into the deep end and get all of their skeletons out of the closet. There is a time and a place for this, but the class meeting is not it. (This will be discussed further in chapter 7.)

One of the key roles of the class leader, then, is to set the tone the first few weeks the group meets by being the first person to answer the question. This helps to put the rest of the group at ease, because the class leader provides a sort of template that the rest of the group will tend to follow. It also provides an invaluable opportunity to provide a helpful model for the entire group. If a class leader is vulnerable and honest, genuinely trying to wrestle with their relationship with God and where things have been good and where there is room for growth, or where there has been a sense of absence or separation from God, the rest of the group will likely follow suit. On the other hand, if the class leader gives superficial, surface level answers and feels that they cannot be vulnerable with the group, but has to posture as a spiritual expert with no struggles, the rest of the group will also struggle to go beneath the surface.

The most important role of the class leader, then, is modeling for the rest of the group how to talk about the state of one's soul.

Qualities of a Class Leader

The best class leaders will be women and men who are willing to be vulnerable with their groups and share openly about their relationships with God. Related to this, they will also be people who have an active relationship with God and are willing and interested in sharing with others the stories of how God's grace has changed them. As such, class leaders will anticipate encountering the Holy Spirit during class meetings. They will expect to see lives changed by the living God.

The most effective class leader will gently guide their group, reminding them that the focal point of the group is paying attention to the ways God has been at work. To do this most effectively, the class leader will be a good listener. They will learn to listen for the promptings of the Holy Spirit as their brothers and sisters in Christ talk about the state of their souls.[5] As class leaders become increasingly sensitive to the Spirit's promptings, they will gain confidence in asking questions or making observations that will help others to better interpret the ways that God is at work in their lives. At the same time, class leaders should not feel that they should always, or even usually, say something in response to other group members. The most effective class leader will talk less over time, because they will empower the rest of the group to care for one another, to "watch over one another in love."

A class leader should seek to be a channel or conductor for God to make God's presence known. The class leader will not take on the burden of making their class meeting a life-changing experience for everyone who attends because their group is so well run and directed. Instead, they will pray daily for the members of their class and they will regularly ask God to be in control of their group, to enable them to be sensitive to the Holy Spirit, and to respond faithfully when prompted by the Spirit. In other words, the most effective class leader will be someone who is desperately dependent on God, rather than depending on themselves, to make the class meeting experience meaningful for all who attend.

At a more basic level, an effective class leader will not, on the one hand, be domineering or unnecessarily authoritarian. On the other hand, she will step in when necessary in order to keep the meeting on track. It is the role of the class leader, for example, to prevent one person from monopolizing the conversation and not giving other group members the chance to speak. It is also the class leader's responsibility to keep the group focused on their relationship with God, rather than becoming a general report on what happened last week. If, for example, someone answers the "How is it with your soul?" question by saying, "I am having a very busy time at work," the class leader might respond with a question like, "How are the challenges you are experiencing at work impacting your relationship with God?" In this way, the class leader helps return the person's focus to their experience of God's work in their life.

What a Class Leader Should *Not* Do

As we wrap up our discussion of a class leader, here are a few things a class leader should *not* do:

First, the class leader should not see himself as a teacher. As has been stressed throughout this book, the class meeting is not an informational approach to the Christian life where the group studies the Bible or other curriculum. One of the roles of the class leader is to resist suggestions that the group would be more effective if it were to shift toward reading a book or focusing on some other material. There are places for studies in the ministries that a church offers, but that is not the focus of this approach to small groups. The class leader, then, should not allow the dynamics of the group to shift to where she becomes the teacher or expert of the group and the rest of the group becomes increasingly passive. On the contrary! The role of the class leader is to empower every person in the group to become increasingly active in his or her discipleship.

Related to this, it is not the class leader's job to have all of the answers. In other words, even in groups that do not formally focus on a study, the class meeting could become a counseling session, where group members bring their struggles to the group with the expectation that the class leader will solve their problems for them. While the class leader may sometimes offer just the right insight to someone at exactly the time they need it, the class leader is not the spiritual guru who solves everyone else's problems. The class leader should see himself as a facilitator, rather than an expert or teacher.

Second, in order to resist the temptation to become the expert of the group, the class leader should not feel the need to respond to every person at every meeting. While the class leader can model the best way to respond to someone by affirming what they have shared, asking further questions of them, or sharing ways that they have approached the same situation, the class leader should not feel as though they always have to have something to say in response to each person. Someone's answer to the question "How is your life in God?" may not always require a response, other than a basic affirmation of what they have shared, and perhaps thanking them for sharing. Other times, the Holy Spirit will use someone else to say exactly the right thing to the person who shared. The most effective class leaders will help others learn how to care for one another by creating space for people to contribute to the group. As a practical matter, class leaders are not selected because they know everything, or because they have all the answers. Rather, each is selected because they have a living relationship with Jesus and are willing to step out in faith and share that journey with others in the hope that God will use it to bless others.

Third, the class leader should not allow the weekly meeting to last more than an hour and a half. While there should be freedom for the Spirit to move, and there may be weeks when it is obvious to everyone that the group is not done meeting when the time to end has come, this should be the exception and not the rule. For some groups, an initial experience of closeness may cause the meetings to tend to become longer and longer. I know of one group that for a few months was consistently meeting for three hours. While it was great that the group was experiencing such closeness and was having such a meaningful experience, this is ultimately not sustainable. In the group I mentioned, the members began to feel burned-out and actually started to dread going to the weekly meeting because they were anticipating how long it was going to last.

Imagine that your class meeting meets at the end of the workday on a Wednesday. You enjoy the people in your group and find it to be a crucial guide to helping you focus on your relationship with God throughout the week. No matter how positive your experience of the group is, there will likely be times when you would rather just go home and relax after a long day. Or if your group meets in the morning, you might rather sleep in. This is an unavoidable dynamic of any small group, but it is significantly increased in a group that meets longer than it should. Ultimately, people will stop coming to the group if it becomes a weekly marathon. The class leader should prevent this from happening by starting and ending the meeting on time.

Finally, the class leader should not allow the group to grow beyond twelve members. Please note that I am *not* saying that the class leader should not allow the group to grow. A key goal of the class meeting is to continually incorporate new people into its life. At some point, since the key purpose of the class meeting is for each person to share the current state of his or her relationship with God, the group dynamic will be impaired if there are too many people in the class. Instead of creating a culture where the group is stagnant and does not invite new people into it, the class leader should encourage the addition of new members to the group and constantly keep an eye out for people who evidence the potential to become excellent class leaders. When this happens, the class leader could ask to meet with this person and ask about their interest in becoming a class leader. In most churches, it will not be the class leader's responsibility to train new class leaders or divide the class. However, they can be an asset to whoever oversees the class meetings as a whole by helping them know when a class meeting is becoming too large to be effective, as well as identifying potential leaders.

A Contemporary Class Leader's Testimony

To conclude this chapter, I would like to let Nick, a class leader at Munger Place Church, again speak for himself about his experience with leading a class meeting (remember that at Munger Place they call their groups "kitchen groups"):

Leading a kitchen group has helped me to recognize that the Holy Spirit is active and is always amazing. . . . I was so nervous the first couple of weeks. My voice shook [because] I wanted them to be blessed by this experience the same way that I have been blessed. . . . [Christ] is present in the lives of our group members today, so we need to hear the ways Christ has been at work in each other's lives. Each believer, strong or struggling, new to the faith or old, brings something to the group each week that someone needs to hear.

We pray each week that the Lord will be amongst us and I have come to realize that God is present, and that no matter how much I try to run a good meeting, no matter how eloquent my prayer might be, etc., the key to the success of the group is the presence of the Holy Spirit. The Holy Spirit is truly active in our group, wanting to bless us with his presence. You cannot convince me otherwise. . . . Sometimes it's the small steps or just the love of someone reaching out and offering some encouragement from shared experience. But I can see it. I see it in the relationships that are being formed, the changes occurring in people's hearts and the resolve of the group to stick it out this time. I have also learned that people long for honest interactions about their faith, doubts, struggles and triumphs.[6]

I hope that you will take the same risk that Nick took and step out in faith to become a class leader. As you do, may you experience the presence and activity of the Holy Spirit, just as Nick has!

Guide for Small Group Discussion

Organization:

:00–:15 Informal Conversation

Open with a Prayer

:15–:50 Questions for Discussion

1. What were your general thoughts or reactions to this chapter? Was anything particularly exciting or challenging to you? Why?

2. Which of the "dos" of a class leader do you think would be the easiest? Which would be the most challenging? Which of the "don'ts" would be the easiest? Which would be the most challenging?

3. What was your reaction to Nick's testimony of his experience with being a class leader? What do you think would be most challenging about being a class leader? What would be most exciting? What might be the potential rewards in taking the risk of leading a class meeting?

4. Most of you are not currently leading a class meeting. How could you use what you learned about leading a class meeting to be a better participant in a class meeting? In other words, how can you make it more likely that the class leader will thrive in leading the group?

:50–1:15 Transformation Question

Moving into leadership of almost any kind can feel like a risk. Can you identify ways that you have experienced God when you have taken a step in faith to take on leadership for which you didn't feel qualified or prepared? Or, can you think of another experience where you took a step in faith that felt risky? What was your experience of God when you took this step?

Close with a Prayer

7

What Could Possibly Go Wrong?

May the time never come when class-meetings shall be
laid aside in the Methodist Episcopal Church.[1]

—Peter Cartwright

If you have much experience with small groups, you probably don't have to think very hard to come up with powerful stories of transformation or hilarious stories of awkward small group experiences. One video on YouTube, "Shallow Small Group," parodies how some small groups can fail to go beyond the surface level, "because when things get too deep, people drown."[2] I will never forget hearing of one ice-breaking exercise that was quite uncomfortable for those who experienced it. A roll of toilet paper was passed around the group (yes, toilet paper!), and each person was told to take the number of squares of toilet paper that they would use in the bathroom. Then each person had to share one thing about themselves for each square of toilet paper taken. I wish I were making this up, but someone actually thought this would be a good idea!

There are many ways to ruin a perfectly good small group, and over the years people have found amazingly creative ways to do just that! In this chapter, we will take a serious look at some of the most common ways that a new class meeting would be likely to fail. To keep things a bit lighter, this chapter will consider the "Top Ten Ways to Guarantee That Your Class Meeting Will Fail."

The goal of this chapter is to identify some of the major things in small group dynamics that can undermine the vitality or long-term success of a group. If you are serious about starting something like a class meeting, you will need to think about how you are going to address some of the challenges that come with starting such a group. Some of the things I will mention can be pretty touchy, and may even make people angry if you call them out on it in the moment. One strategy that can help the group be aware of some of these dangers is to name them before they become a problem. There is a decent chance on any given day that nearly everyone in the group will struggle with at least one of these things. Finally, humor can be a way to address serious things in a way that people can hear more easily. So, talking about how to guarantee the failure of a class meeting can be a disarming way to name some things that might make people feel a bit defensive. So, here we go:

Top Ten Ways to Guarantee That Your Class Meeting Will Fail

#10. Never Start One

This one is pretty straightforward. The easiest way to guarantee that your class meeting will fail is to talk about starting a class meeting, to seriously consider it, but to never actually start one. While the reason that this is a strategy for failure is obvious, it is actually a major reason why many class meetings never get off the ground. As I have spoken in local churches and at conferences about the early Methodist class meeting and the potential value that could come from reclaiming this practice today, I have been surprised at how quickly people have bought my argument. It has not been difficult to convince local church leaders that returning to something similar to the class meeting would be more likely to help people grow in their relationship with Jesus Christ than the ministries that the local church typically offers.

However, it is sometimes easier to stay in the abstract or theoretical than to get down to the practical details of actually doing something. A deep motivation of this book is to provide local church leaders a resource they can use to actually start class meetings. And if this book accomplishes its purpose, the vast majority of you are reading it as part of your participation in a small group that is preparing to become an actual class meeting. In fact, if you are using the "Guide for Small Group Discussion" at the end of each chapter during your time together as a group, then you are already well on your way to not just preparing to become a class meeting, but to *being* a class meeting. You are already starting to have significant conversations together about the states of your souls and your experience of God's presence in your lives.

I hope you will press on, that you will continue to take the risk of entering into one another's lives in the hope that as a group you will become more and more committed to your faith and to helping one another grow as followers of Jesus Christ. I hope this will not be merely another study *about* something that fails to change your lives. Rather, my prayer is that this will help you *be transformed* through committing to this practice. Through committing to do this, you will find that you are increasingly aware of God's work in your life, and you will begin to anticipate encountering God every day. The first step, particularly if you are not reading this within the context of a new class meeting, then, is to take action and move from the theoretical to the concrete by starting a class meeting.

#9. Meet Irregularly

My wife and I volunteered to host a class meeting in our apartment when I was a PhD student. One of the first weeks that the group met, there was a schedule change that came up a few days before one of the group meetings. We e-mailed and called every group member for which we had contact information. We thought we had communicated with every person in the group, but we evidently failed because right when the group was supposed to have started, someone rang our doorbell. I think we had just sat down to eat dinner. I remember feeling terrible that she had wasted her time driving to our apartment. We also barely knew each other, which made it that much more awkward. To her credit, she came back the next week and we quickly put it behind us. But for some people who are already taking a significant step outside of their comfort zone, that kind of misstep would be enough for them to decide not to come to the group in the future.

So, you can guarantee that your class meeting will fail if you meet on an unpredictable schedule, or frequently change times or locations. It is probably obvious, but if you decide to meet at an inconvenient or irregular time for the current group members, the time that the group meets will guarantee that some people will not participate (because their schedules do not allow them to). I have been part of groups that have tried to meet on irregular schedules, and in my experience the group has always dwindled over time. When a group does not meet regularly, people drop out for two main reasons: (1) They simply forget that the group was meeting and so forget to come to the meeting. This could be partially offset by the class leader proactively communicating with the group, perhaps sending out a reminder e-mail a day or two before the meeting. (2) They are confused as to whether or not the group is meeting, which provides enough of a reason for some people to not come, particularly those who are just starting to feel some commitment to the group. Again, this could be partially offset by proactive communication. Nevertheless, in my experience small groups are stronger when they meet once a week at the same time and at the same place.

Related to this, some groups decide to change locations from one week to another in order to offset the burden of hosting the group. This idea arises for a number of very good reasons. However, I ultimately think it is a strategy that is more likely to produce failure than success because it creates further confusion for people who may not be as organized as you are. The reality is that most people keep pretty full schedules, and not everyone does a great job of keeping up with everything that they have going on. As an act of hospitality, then, class meetings should meet in the same place every week. If group members want to do something to offset the work that hosting the group requires, other group members could take turns providing light refreshments (if that is a part of the group). In general, successful class meetings meet every week at the same time, on the same day, and in the same location.

#8. Turn the Class Meeting into a Curriculum-Driven Group

I know, I know. It sounds as if I am starting to beat a dead horse here. But I've often been told that repetition helps with retention! The best way to guarantee that your class meeting will fail is to turn it into a curriculum-driven group. As we discussed in chapter 5, small groups often have a life cycle of their own. After people gain some level of comfort with the class meeting, perhaps at around three to six months of meeting, and it establishes a routine, people may become restless and wonder what is next. At this stage, where the group is questioning and refining its purpose, a well-intentioned person may suggest that the group read and discuss a book they just read that really inspired and challenged them in their walk with God. If and when this happens, there needs to be a gentle stubbornness by the group, and particularly the class leader. All members should insist that the group not become a study group. Bible studies and other study groups are not bad, but they are not class meetings. For a class to succeed today, the group needs to have a deep commitment that the purpose of the group is to take a weekly inventory of how things are going in each person's life with God.

It is fine for group members to share things they have read that have inspired them, that have been particularly convicting, or that helped them gain a sense of God's direction in their lives. It is also fine for group members to recommend a book that someone else might find helpful because of something that they shared. However, the group should not shift to becoming a study unless the group chooses to self-consciously reject the argument this book makes and return to an informational approach to the Christian life. Rather than becoming an information-driven group, I would encourage people who become restless as the group becomes a bit more settled into a routine to give the group more time and to realize that sometimes what appears to be stagnation can be seen in retrospect to have been used by God to bring growth. Sometimes the Holy Spirit uses discomfort to draw us closer to the Father.

#7. Make the Class Meeting an Intense Accountability Group

One way to guarantee the failure of your class meeting is to try to make it more than it is. Class meetings are groups that have both men and women, married and single folks together in the same group. These groups are designed to be accessible to everyone, even to people who are just beginning to explore the possibility of a relationship with God. Class meetings are not accountability groups; they are not places where people confess their deepest sins to one another.

In early Methodism, there was actually a group that was smaller than the class meeting (it typically had three to six people), and it was divided by gender and marital status. These groups were called *band meetings*.[3] To join a band meeting, one had to have a prior experience of justification by faith in Christ and assurance of one's new birth as a child of God. The key activity of the band meeting was the confession of any sins that had been committed in the past week, including the ways that people had been tempted to sin. The purpose of these groups was to bring sin into the light, to express repentance of these sins, to encourage one another to move from sin toward God and holiness by the grace of God. Band meetings were an intense form of accountability and required deep vulnerability. I think that something like the band meeting could be of tremendous value to contemporary Christianity; however, people should be given a clear and accurate description of what they are committing to. If people think they are joining a class, but it functions like a band meeting, they will likely feel that they are in over their heads. Further, there is a greater degree of spiritual maturity required of the band than there is in the class meeting, so if people jump straight into the bands before they are ready, a host of issues can arise.

#6. Select the Class Leader Based on Anything Other than Spiritual Maturity and Spiritual Leadership

We have already discussed the key role of the class leader (see chapter 6) and how crucial their leadership is to the success of the class meeting. It is essential to have a mature Christian as the leader of the class meeting, because the leader is the one who will gently move the conversation on as needed, ensure that every person has a chance to talk, and otherwise facilitate the meeting. The leader will guide the group through its development and through challenges the group may face. This person will also set the tone for the group by being the first one to answer the question, "How is your life with God?" every week and by keeping the group focused on its purpose.

Because of the qualities the ideal class leader will possess, however, the best class leaders may not necessarily be the people who would immediately come to mind for a host of other leadership positions in the church. To use leadership terms in Methodist congregations, the chair of staff parish relations, the administrative council chair, and the finance committee chair are not necessarily the right persons to lead a class meeting. The class leader should be chosen because they are able and willing to talk about their relationship with God and because they show an ability to encourage others in their relationships with God. And again, if a church is passionate about its members becoming disciples, or deeply committed followers of Jesus Christ, the priority of the church should be *first* identifying who the best class leaders would be, and then filling the rest of the positions in the church. After all, it doesn't really matter who is keeping track of the finances of the church if no one in the church is becoming a deeply committed follower of Jesus Christ!

#5. Allow One Person to Dominate the Conversation

My guess is that this is one that basically every group will struggle with. For one thing, this type of small group will be most comfortable for people who like to talk and who process things by talking about them. This is one area that is particularly important to address up front. At the beginning of a new class meeting, the leader should stress that it is important that every person be given the opportunity to talk. The leader may even want to acknowledge that some people talk more easily than others, and that these folks may need to challenge themselves to be more concise and aware of how long they have been talking. On the other hand, those who are less comfortable talking may need to challenge themselves to talk a bit more. If this is addressed up front, then it will not seem as personal if the leader gently suggests that the conversation needs to move to the next person during a meeting.

If someone unintentionally dominates the conversation, the leader should *not* say, "You have been talking for too long; let's move on." When someone talks too long, even though everyone else may be suffering over how long they have been talking, the person who is actually talking usually has no idea how long it has been. The best approach is to gently interrupt them by thanking them for sharing, briefly identifying one thing they have said that was particularly appreciated, and then simply asking the next person the question, "How is it with your soul?" or "How is your life in God?" The person who is interrupted may feel embarrassed, but if the leader moves the attention to someone else, the embarrassed group member won't have the double embarrassment of having the attention still focused on them.

By the way, this one hits pretty close to home for me, because I am one of those who processes things by talking. As a result, I have to really work to be aware of how long I have been talking. I also have to work on being concise. One other practical strategy

I have found that has helped me is to position myself so that I would be the last person to share. If I am last and there are only two minutes left when it is my turn, then I have to make do with the time that is left. It also guarantees that other folks in the group get their fair share of time to talk.

#4. Have All of the Answers

This is a catch-all for several ways to ruin a class meeting. In small group dynamics there is often an expert who emerges in the group. You probably know what I am talking about, someone who has all the answers. This person is the only person who fails to realize when a rhetorical question has been asked. To them, every question has an answer. And they always know what the answer is. These people also have the best of intentions. They are passionate about their faith and are eager to share what they have learned with others. They really believe they are helping. However, one of the best ways to stifle a conversation is by being a know-it-all. Other people in the group will be less likely to be vulnerable and share doubts, anxieties, or concerns that they are having if there is one person who always has everything figured out and leaves no room for other people to be in flux, or working through things.

Another way this can manifest in a group is if the leader sees herself as a teacher, not a facilitator. This can be deadly, because if the leader is the one causing the problem, it will be very difficult for the group to overcome. So, if you are involved in starting something like a class meeting, please know that it is not your job to have a solution to every problem that people in your class raise. You are there to walk with the people in your group as they seek God's transforming grace. And you are there because you need them to walk with you as you seek God's transforming grace in your own life.

One more thing: if you have been in a lot of small groups and have never noticed that this is sometimes a problem of small group dynamics—you might be the one with all the answers!

#3. Hide During the Meeting

I don't mean literally hiding, like behind the sofa, although that would certainly be a problem too! By hiding I mean either not talking or not being honest about what is really going on in your life with God. This doesn't mean that the class meeting is the place for you to bring up the darkest parts of your past. In fact, it is *not* the place for that.

Members who have had a bad week may be tempted to gloss over their struggles by saying that things have been fine, or okay. If you are in a class meeting for an extended period of time, you will almost certainly have weeks where it is NOT well with your soul. It is okay to be honest about that. In fact, it is vital for the future wellness of your soul to be honest when things are not going well. When you are struggling in your faith, this is the time when the class meeting may be the biggest means of grace in your life. If you are honest, you will realize you are not alone. You will receive sympathy and prayers from the group. And in verbalizing your spiritual malaise, you may learn more about what is going on below the surface in your relationship with God.

Related to this, there is sometimes a tendency in class meetings to feel as though you have to one-up yourself every week. This is particularly unhelpful because it can become a sort of disease that spreads throughout the group. If you are already the hero in the story of your Christian walk, others may not feel that they have room to struggle. When things are going well, don't hide your joy in what the Lord is doing for you or in you. And if things are not going well, try to resist the temptation to gloss over your struggles. If you are honest and real, you will put yourself in a better position to grow in your relationship with Jesus and you will be far more likely to be used by God to bless someone else in your group. One of the wonderful things about the class meeting is that it is a place where every person can grow where he or she is.

#2. View the Group as a Place to Gather Gossip

One of the best ways to guarantee that your class meeting will fail is by breaking the confidence of the group. It needs to be clearly said that what is shared in the class meeting is confidential. The things that are discussed in the class meeting are not legitimate topics of conversation with friends or even family members outside of the group. If there is some reason that talking with someone else might be helpful to the person who shared, what was said in the group can only be shared with someone outside of the group if the person who shared the information gives their permission. You should assume that everything that is said in the context of the class meeting is confidential unless you are explicitly told otherwise.

There may not be anything that can be more harmful to a class meeting than a feeling of mistrust among the group members about whether confidence will be kept in the group. If you struggle to keep secrets, or to keep things to yourself, the class meeting may not be for you. Confidentiality is *not* optional!

Some of you may be reading this a bit too quickly and not allowing this to really sink in. Please hear me carefully. An inability to keep something in confidence is a deep character flaw and a sign of immaturity. If you choose to violate the confidence of your group, here is what you are doing: (1) You are breaking a promise that you made to the group. (2) You are saying that your right to share information is more important than the other person's right to ask you not to share it. In other words, you are saying that you are more important than the other members of your group. You are putting your needs above those of a brother or sister in Christ. (3) You are choosing to do something that will destroy the chemistry of the entire group, even doing lasting damage to people's relationships with Christ. I'm not kidding. I am amazed at how often I hear people say that they left the church because of backbiting and being hurt by gossip. (4) You are making it far less likely that people will share confidential things in the future, possibly keeping someone from sharing something that could be really important to his or her growth as a Christian.

Please don't gossip. It is a sin, and it is a particularly deadly sin when it is a violation of the trust that is built in a class meeting.

#1. Be Unwilling to Be Challenged to Grow in Your Faith and Be Transformed by the Grace of God

The class meeting is an invaluable asset for people who desire to grow in their faith and seek to be transformed by the grace of God. When people gather together to support and encourage one another, God will also be there. The class meeting, however, is not for those who do not want to be changed. It is not for those who are content to profess faith in God the Father, Son, and Holy Spirit on Sunday morning and then live the rest of the week as if there is no God. The class meeting is for those who are desperate to know God more deeply and to grow in their relationship with the Father, Son, and Holy Spirit.

Nearly in the Top Ten: Meet for More Than an Hour and a Half

As mentioned in chapter 6, class meetings can sometimes meet longer than they are supposed to because something exciting is happening in the group. Someone may have a breakthrough, and the group wants to allow them to process it. This is okay if it happens occasionally. However, it should be rare. If a weekly meeting consistently lasts longer than an hour and a half, people will begin to feel exhausted just by the thought of going to the group. The group leader should remember that a commitment to attend a group once a week for one to one and a half hours is already a major time commitment. Leaders should work to formally end the meeting on time by closing with a prayer. Conversation can certainly continue among those who wish to stay, or talk at their cars. But formally ending the meeting gives those who need to leave the opportunity to do so.

Ultimately, We Are Not in Control, but the Spirit Is

All the concerns about what might go wrong cannot be addressed in advance. We are messy people. We are good at sinning. Something could go wrong. In fact, something probably will go wrong. But if we believe that the Holy Spirit is active and present with us, we don't have to have everything mapped out in advance. We should be prudent in doing what we can to make a group like a class meeting as likely to succeed and be a blessing to its members as possible. However, we should also leave room for the Spirit to guide and direct each meeting. In fact, you should pray for the Holy Spirit to show up in recognizable ways every time your group meets, guiding and directing the meeting and each person's life in between meetings.

I believe that the Spirit of God wants to use these types of groups to bring real transformation and healing to people's lives. Contemporary class meetings will ultimately succeed, not because of the determination or competence of the leader or the individuals in the group. Rather, they will succeed because God wills them to. This is not to say that preparation and forethought are irrelevant. They matter, and we should do what we can to facilitate the Spirit's work through us. But we should also remind ourselves that we are not, and cannot be, the source of our own transformation. Sanctification is a sheer act of grace. We cannot earn it or merit it. It is freely given to us by the triune God. One of the most basic and profound things that these groups can help us to do is to remind us to look to God for salvation, instead of trying to save ourselves.

Guide for Small Group Discussion

Note that the time for discussion is decreased by an additional five minutes this week and five minutes are added to the discussion of the Transformation Question.

Organization:

:00–:15 Informal Conversation

Open with a Prayer

:15–:45 Questions for Discussion

1. What were your general thoughts or reactions to this chapter? Was anything particularly exciting or challenging to you? Why?
2. Which of the "Top Ten Ways to Guarantee That Your Class Meeting Will Fail" do you think would be the deadliest to a class meeting? Why?
3. Which one of these is the most difficult for you personally?
4. What would you add to this list? That is, what else do you think would be particularly harmful to the dynamics of a class meeting? Or, what should we be proactive about avoiding?

:45–1:15 Transformation Question

Another way to guarantee that your class meeting will fail is if you never get around to answering the basic question of the class meeting. So, this week we take a test run at answering the basic class meeting question. Try to speak for 2–3 minutes about your sense of where you are currently in your relationship with God:

How is your life in God? If it helps, you can name specific places where you have seen God at work in your life over the past week.

Close with a Prayer

8

The Keys to a Life-Changing Group

*In these class-meetings many seekers of religion
have found them the spiritual birth-place of their
souls into the heavenly family, and their dead souls
made alive to God.*[1]

—Peter Cartwright

In chapter 4, we read an extended quotation from Peter Cartwright, a nineteenth-century American Methodist preacher, where he discussed the crucial role the class meeting had played in early Methodism, and lamented its decline. In particular, Cartwright described the ways he had seen God use the class meeting:

In these class-meetings the weak have been made strong; the bowed down have been raised up; the tempted have found delivering grace; the doubting mind has had all its doubts and fears removed; and the whole class have found that this was "none other than the house of God, and the gate of heaven." Here the hard heart has been tendered, the cold heart warmed with holy fire; here the dark mind, beclouded with trial and temptation, has had every cloud rolled away, and the sun of righteousness has risen with resplendent glory, "with healing in his wings;" and in these class-meetings many seekers of religion have found them the spiritual birth-place of their souls into the heavenly family, and their dead souls made alive to God.[2]

The goal of this book (despite what the last chapter may have suggested) is not to show you how to destroy a perfectly good class meeting. Rather, it is to introduce you to a practice that has the potential to strengthen your life in Christ, help you be delivered from temptation, and help those who are seeking Jesus to find new life in him. Cartwright, like Wesley, was convinced that a relationship with Jesus was best experienced and most likely to grow within the context of community, a "heavenly family."

With the hope, by God's grace, of preparing you to begin meeting regularly as a class meeting from this point forward, this chapter brings the book to a conclusion by outlining a few keys to a life-changing small group. The chapter first discusses the characteristics of a group that God can use to bring deep change and healing to people's lives. It then describes the qualities you should seek in order to make it most likely that God can use such a group to draw you closer.

A Group That God Can Use to Bring Life Change

At the very beginning of this book, I argued that not all small groups are equal—some are better than others. Small groups that focus on information (curriculum-driven studies) tend to draw people's attention away from who they are in Christ and are not as successful in helping people become more like Christ. So, what characteristics would make a group most likely to succeed in transforming the lives of its members?

Back to the Basics

One of the most important keys to the success of any type of small group involves basic organization and planning. A life-changing group will be made up of members who plan for the group to succeed by agreeing on a regular time and place to meet, intentionally carving out space for the group in their lives, and committing to attend the group consistently.

As I have previously said, the group should plan to meet weekly at a specific time and place. This helps to avoid confusion and worry about when the group is meeting. It also makes it easier for attending the group to become a regular part of your life, for it to become a habit. It is common for small groups to decide to meet every other week, rather than every week. Though it is better for a group to meet every other week than not at all, the group is more likely to become a deep part of the rhythm of your life if it meets every week. Most of our lives are structured around the rhythm of a seven-day week, and so the class meeting has the best chance of success if it becomes a part of your weekly routine.

It is not enough, however, for the group to commit to meeting every week at a regular time and place. The members of the group also need to commit to be there every time the group meets. Remember, this group is not an information-driven group. It is a place for sharing what is happening in one's life as a follower of Jesus Christ, with the hope that God's grace will transform one's life in deep and lasting ways. If you miss a meeting, then, you are not just missing interesting information that you can make up at another time. You are missing an opportunity to walk with someone else as they seek to grow closer to God. You are missing an opportunity to grow closer to Jesus yourself. And you are missing an opportunity to be a part of a group of people who have committed to watch over one another in love.

Consistency is not just important; it is *necessary* for a group like this to accomplish its goal of helping people's lives be transformed by the living God. If you are not consistent in attending the group, you will miss out on the benefits that come from being a part of the group. Perhaps more important, your sporadic attendance may harm the dynamics of the group itself. As the group naturally grows in intimacy and comfort with each other, your inconsistent attendance would interrupt the dynamics of the rest of the group.

My point here is not that someone should never come to the group again if they miss one time. But inconsistent attendance does send a message to the rest of the group, communicating that the group is not a major priority for the person whose attendance is inconsistent. It also conveys that investing in the lives of these other people is only something I am willing to do when it is convenient for me. You will (justifiably) be less likely to be vulnerable and open with me if you are not convinced that I really care about you and what is going on in your life.

Cultivating Self-Awareness

During the first undergraduate class I taught at Seattle Pacific University, I was taken aback by the number of students who texted throughout the class. I initially ignored the texting, but it became increasingly frustrating to me as the class continued. I eventually confronted the class, because I realized that the students were communicating disrespect not only for me but for the other students in the class. Now, on the first day of a new class, I ask students not to send text messages during class. And I tell them that if I see them texting, I will count them absent because if they are communicating with someone outside of class, they are not really present *in class*.

The key point here is that showing up to a group meeting is important, but not sufficient for the best experience. In order for you to have the best experience, and for the rest of the group to benefit from the insights you bring to the group, you need to be physically and mentally present. One of the most important skills for a thriving class meeting is listening. You can't listen to someone else talk about the ways they have experienced God's presence in the past week if you are messing with your cell phone. It may sound overly rigid, but I would strongly encourage group members to turn their cell phones off during the time the class is meeting.

Listening is not simply being quiet while someone else is talking. The best listeners are active listeners. They do not merely avoid interrupting; they give cues that show they are listening and interested, such as nodding their heads or smiling when appropriate. As you gain experience and comfort in listening to others talk about their relationships with God, you may find that you ask questions of the person who is sharing because of nonverbal cues you pick up on as often as you ask questions because of things they state explicitly. How someone says something is often as important as what is said!

Interpersonal skills are essential to a life-changing class meeting. Beyond listening carefully to one another, group members should convey respect and care for each other. This means that group members should think about the other people in their group and value their experiences in the group. Attentiveness to the experience of the rest of the group will also help you avoid extremes, such as dominating the conversation or remaining completely detached. In an exceptional class meeting, group members will be self-aware. They will think about how they communicate and how to more effectively and appropriately communicate within the context of the class meeting.

Life-changing groups will have members who honor the promise of confidentiality that is made in each group. Members will recognize that violating the confidence of the group is breaking a commitment that has been made and that people will not feel safe being honest and vulnerable in a group if one member talks to outsiders about what is said in the group. I know I am repeating myself here, but this is a serious enough concern that it is worth repeating. If you cannot respect requests for confidentiality, then you should not be a part of a group like this.

Finally, a group that is most likely to be used by God to bring life change will consist of members who cultivate humility and a willingness to be vulnerable with the group. Humility is a powerful trait in a small group, but it is often misunderstood to mean feeling that you have no wisdom or experience to offer the group. Humility is better understood to entail detachment from your own strengths and weaknesses, while possessing a realistic appreciation of them. In other words, a humble person is *not* someone who acts as if they do not have a gift that they clearly possess. Rather, they offer the gift to others with a sense that it is not something that they own.

C. S. Lewis offered one of my favorite definitions of humility: "[God] wants to bring the man to a state of mind in which he could design the best cathedral in the world, and know it to be the best, and rejoice in the fact, without being any more (or less) or otherwise glad at having done it than he would be if it had been done by another."[3] If God has gifted you with the ability to lead a class meeting with wisdom and discernment that benefits the entire group, you should claim that gift and rejoice in what God is doing in the group. Similarly, humble people will not chastise themselves for not having a particular gift, but rejoice that the gifts needed for the entire group to thrive have been given to the group as a whole.

Vulnerability is related to humility. It takes vulnerability to admit your own limitations, particularly if they are related to an area of personal embarrassment or shame. A willingness to be vulnerable is also necessary for a successful group, as a class meeting will only go as far as the members in the group are willing to let the Spirit take them. If you are going through a difficult period in your life with God and you are unwilling to be honest with the group about it, your unwillingness to be vulnerable may hinder the extent to which the group can help you regain a sense of the Spirit's active presence in your life. Vulnerability is necessary because the content of the class meeting is your experience of God's work in your life, discussing this with others can sometimes make you feel vulnerable. But this is the best kind of vulnerability, because it leads to growth.

Much more could be said about the importance of cultivating self-awareness. The key principle, however, is that a group will be dynamic and powerful if every member seeks to be aware of the ways that his or her own presence and ways of communicating impact the other members of the group.

Hospitable to and Eager for New Life

Life-changing small groups are open and welcoming to new life. At first glance this may seem trivial or even suspect to you. Why would bringing new people in be essential to the vitality of a small group? On the contrary, couldn't bringing new people into a group do the very opposite—make it unstable and decrease intimacy and vulnerability?

This book is not a cookbook. I cannot give you a recipe to follow step-by-step (sprinkle in a prayer, add a dash of conversation about God's work in your life, bake for three months, add a new member, etc.) that will guarantee a particular outcome. Class meetings are both more fragile and more powerful than a formula. There may be times when it is not prudent to add new members to the group. (In fact, I would not recommend adding new members to a group until it has sufficient history to have become well established in the routine phase described in chapter 5.) Too much instability can be harmful.

On the other hand, a healthy group will always seek to give what it has found to others. I was surprised and disheartened recently to hear a church make a distinction between small groups that were "open groups" and "closed groups," with no sense of concern about these categories. While class meetings should not be open to people to simply come and go, with no commitment to the group, a group should generally be open to new life. In fact, the groups that are most likely to change the lives of their members will also be the groups that are the most eager to include people who don't even know they are in need of a group like this yet.

A Group That God Can Use to Change *Your* Life

The previous section discussed some of the qualities of a group that will make it most likely to bring life change to its members. Another way of putting this is that the last section discussed the dynamics that make a group most likely to be impactful. This section puts the focus squarely on you and asks: What qualities can you bring that will make it most likely that God will use this group to bring transformation and real growth in holiness to your life? Wesleyans believe that God does not drag anyone kicking and screaming to holiness. Particularly in twenty-first-century American Christianity, which often seems to value comfort and the felt needs of the individual above all else, our need for healing and transformation as a sheer act of God's amazing grace is often overlooked or ignored. Books like this one always run the risk of being yet one more way that we try to make ourselves good enough, when the truth is that we cannot be the source of our own healing.

Take Responsibility for Your Faith

The triune God—Father, Son, and Holy Spirit—is the only one who is able to heal us of our addiction to sin and our love of comfort more than discipleship. The basic conviction of this study, however, is that God is *able and willing* to restore us to health. God is the initiator and the primary actor. But God also invites us to participate in the Spirit's work in our lives.

There are many things that the ministries of the church can offer to people. One thing they cannot do is make people take responsibility for their own relationship with God. As the well-worn cliché goes, "You can lead a horse to water, but you can't make him drink." One of the main reasons Sunday school was detrimental to American Methodism was because it encouraged people to look to someone else to take ownership for their faith. The Sunday school provided the answers you needed to know, and in many ways people could even begin to look to the curricular approach to tell them which questions to ask (for a review, see chapter 4).

John Wesley was adamant that God has provided a litany of ways that people who were seeking Christ could reliably expect to find nourishment. Wesley would be appalled at the contemporary idea that all one needs to do to be a Christian is to show up at church and get fed. The point is not that the church is not valuable. On the contrary, it has been entrusted with stewarding many of the key means of grace, like the public worship of God, the Eucharist, and baptism. Rather, the key to a small group that is most likely to change your life is *you* and your decision to take ownership of your faith, to not be passive but active in your commitment to take up your cross and follow Jesus.

If you are serious about participating in God's work of renewal in your life, you will commit to do the things that disciples of Jesus Christ do: read Scripture regularly, spend time in prayer by yourself and with others, worship with others who are seeking to follow Christ, receive the Lord's Supper (which Wesley referred to as the "grand channel" of God's grace), give generously of your time and money, and serve others.

I believe that reclaiming the class meeting has greater potential than anything else I can think of to help the Wesleyan/ Methodist branch of Christianity again become a movement that has the form *and* power of godliness. However, class meetings in eighteenth-century Methodism assumed that members were practicing the basics just mentioned. If you are not willing to commit to reading Scripture daily, praying, etc., then you may need to take a closer look at how serious you really are about your faith in Christ.

Imagine what the response would be to someone who said that they wanted to be a professional baseball player but were not interested in buying a glove. Or someone who said they wanted to write a book but were not willing to spend time writing.

As has often been said, Christians are made, not born. Being a Christian involves a commitment to a basic set of practices. This is the foundation of Christian discipleship. It is of particular relevance for thinking about the class meeting because if you are not serious about your own faith, then you won't have anything of substance to bring with you to the group. The class meeting is *not* a substitute for daily commitment to learning how to practice your faith. It is a wonderful discipline that can help you reinterpret your life through the lens of God's grace, learn how to better discern how God is at work in your life, and give voice to the ways God is at work.

Desire and Expect to Be Changed by God's Grace

A group that is most likely to be used by God to turn your life upside down—for the glory of God—is one in which the participants expect to encounter God in their time together. In such a group, people will be thirsting for transformation by the grace of God, even desperate for it.

This means that we need to recognize our deep need for God's grace. A class meeting (or anything else) is not likely to bring deep change to your life if you do not want to change or do not think change is needed. One of the main things holding back contemporary Christianity is our tendency to be satisfied with who we are (we aren't *that* bad) and our instinctive reliance upon ourselves instead of on God.

Class meetings will be dangerous for the kingdom of God (in a good way!) when they are filled with individual people who refuse to settle for an "okay" life, but instead are desperate to be filled with the presence of the living God. You don't have to be able to articulate exactly why change is needed, or even what is wrong. But you do need to want to become holy, and you need to expect to encounter the One who is able to make you holy.

Show Up!

It is obvious, I know. But the significance of simply showing up for the group whether you feel like it or not should not be underestimated. One of the deep insights behind Wesley's understanding of basic Christian practices is that one of the most important keys to growth in the Christian life is consistently putting yourself in a position where you can be renewed by God's grace.

Showing up is basic to success in many aspects of life, like parenting. It is interesting (and telling) to notice the great lengths to which some people will go to make sure they don't miss their favorite television program or sporting event and how easily they will make excuses for missing something related to their faith, like attending church or a small group.

The principle here is simple: God cannot use a class meeting to change your life if you aren't there!

Conclusion

This chapter has discussed the ways that the most effective small groups are healthy at the group level. Life-changing small groups do little things well, like plan to meet at a regular time and place. Life-changing small groups are also made up of healthy individuals. The people who make up dynamic groups are self-aware, thoughtful, honest, and good listeners. They honor confidentiality, are willing to be vulnerable, and bring a humble spirit to the group. They are also open to new life, seeking to welcome new people into the group. Finally, people in life-changing small groups take ownership of their own faith, not expecting another person to feed them or make them mature Christians. As a result, they invest in their relationships with God on a daily basis and are hungry and thirsty for God, desperate to know the Father, Son, and Holy Spirit more and more deeply and to be more faithful instruments of the Holy Spirit in the world.

By the grace of God, all of these things are possible for your group and for your own life—may it be so!

Guide for Small Group Discussion

Organization:

:00–:15 Informal Conversation

Open with a Prayer

:15–:45 Questions for Discussion

1. What were your general thoughts or reactions to this chapter? Was anything particularly exciting or challenging to you? Why?

2. Do you have a previous experience with a small group that was particularly formative for your life? If so, what was it about the group that made it so powerful?

3. The chapter mentions that curriculum-driven groups sometimes determine not only what information people should be given, but what questions should be asked. What questions do you have based on this chapter's content?

4. This is the last chapter of the book (but don't forget to read the concluding exhortation!). The book has repeatedly stated that the main goal is to help you actually form a class meeting, not merely learn about the class meeting. Spend some time discussing with each other your sense of whether God is calling you to continue meeting as a class meeting. Is this a step the group is willing to take?

:45–1:15 Transformation Question

> How is your life in God? How have you felt God's presence in the past week? Or, where are you seeking guidance from the Lord?

Close with a Prayer

A Concluding Exhortation

As I worked on this book, I was reminded repeatedly of two things:

First, starting a Wesleyan class meeting is actually not that hard. The most important ingredient of a successful class meeting is a group of people who are willing to invest in each other's lives and who are desperate to grow in their relationship with Jesus. Really. All you have to do is commit to meet together to pray and talk about your pursuit of Christ together. I am confident that where people join together to enter more deeply into a relationship with the triune God, the Holy Spirit will not fail to provide the needed guidance and direction. So, as you begin meeting as a class meeting without a book, relax! It isn't that hard. God is with you!

Second, as this book comes to a close, I feel compelled to state clearly that the class meeting is not an end in itself. The goal of the class meeting is to help people come to know and experience God's grace in deeper ways. Indeed, this (being transformed by the grace of God) ought to be the litmus test of everything Christians do. My passion for reclaiming the class meeting is not because I want to see Christians look more like eighteenth-century Methodists. I believe that the class meeting is of continued relevance for Christians because it will be used by God today to help people grow in their faith in Christ.

Not too long ago, I felt deep disappointment and discouragement over the current state of the denomination in which I am ordained. There was a moment when I felt as if no matter how hard people with good intentions tried, something about the structure of the institution made positive change impossible. It felt as though the institution were just too broken to be fixed. And instead of looking to the Holy Spirit for a solution, it felt as if we were still placing our hope in ourselves.

As I was having these thoughts, another thought intruded. It was quiet, yet forceful and clear. *Is this where God wants me to be? Am I called to a place of despair and hopelessness?* These questions were like a pinpoint of light in the darkness, or a drop of water to my parched soul. Immediately, I felt in my soul that the answer to both was "No!" The next question shifted my attention away from the abstract to the concrete: "Is there really nothing that Methodism can do that would help people experience the power of God in their lives?" Again, the answer cut through the confusion, frustration, and despair over a vague and uncertain future.

They could start class meetings.

It may seem naive or overly simplistic, and perhaps it is. But if there is one grand experiment that contemporary Wesleyan communities could try that I believe would be most likely to make disciples of Jesus Christ, it would be attempting to return to the practice of the early Methodist class meeting. That night, as I sat in front of my computer, I imagined a network of a thousand class meetings formed over the next four years. My heart began to race with excitement at the thought, because I knew (and still believe!) that lives would be changed in wonderful ways if thousands of people who have not previously experienced the best of Christian community got a taste of it. The best thing about a vision like this is that I am keenly aware that this is not something I can do on my own! If it is of God, it will happen because the Spirit wills it to happen. And if it is just my idea, it won't.

Please don't misunderstand me; I am not saying that I believe this is the key to saving a denomination. I'm not sure it would. I am not clear on what God's plans are for my denomination, or any other.

I believe I am saying something that is actually much more important than saving a denomination. I am talking about people created in the image of God being renewed in the image in which they were created! I am talking about groups that midwife life-changing encounters with the Holy Spirit! I am praying for God to do for us, yet again, what we cannot do for ourselves. We cannot revive ourselves. But we can join together and pray. We can join together and repent. We can join together and wrestle with where God is already at work in our lives and how we can best join in the work that the Spirit is doing.

I am praying for the Holy Spirit to raise up a network of class meetings throughout the Wesleyan/Methodist family. I believe that if we become so desperate for an encounter with the living God that we are willing to try something new, even uncomfortable, the Spirit will do incredible things.

Are you with me? Will you join a group like this? Will you start one? Will you lead one?

I pray that if this is God's will for you, the Holy Spirit will enable you to say yes.

In the name of the Father, Son, and Holy Spirit, amen.

Notes

Chapter 1

1. Frederick A. Norwood, ed., *The Doctrines and Discipline of the Methodist Episcopal Church, in America. With Explanatory Notes by Thomas Coke and Francis Asbury*, Facsimile ed. (Evanston, IL: The Institute for the Study of Methodism and Related Movements, Garrett-Evangelical Theological Seminary, 1979), 147 (henceforth, *1798 Doctrines and Discipline*).
2. Accessed April 23, 2012.
3. For the full Towers Watson survey, see David de Wetter et al., *UMC Call to Action: Vital Congregations Research Project* (June 28, 2010), http://www.umc.org/atf/cf/%7Bdb6a45e4-c446-4248-82c8-e131b6424741%7D/CV_PRESENTATION.PDF (accessed April 23, 2012).
4. Richard Byrd Wilke and Julia Kitchens Wilke, *Disciple: Becoming Disciples Through Bible Study*, 2nd ed. (Nashville: Abingdon, 1993).
5. This phrase comes from John Wesley. See John Wesley, "The Nature, Design, and General Rules of the United Societies," in *The Works of John Wesley, Bicentennial Edition* (Nashville, TN: Abingdon, 1989), 9:69 (henceforth, John Wesley, "General Rules," in *Works*). All citations preserve the emphases of the original source, unless otherwise noted.
6. For more on Munger Place and their Kitchen Groups, see http://www.mungerplace.org/grouplife/ (accessed March 28, 2013).

7. Nick Weatherford, guest blog post, see http://vitalpiety.com/2011 /02/21/hearing-from-a-21st-century-class-leader-part-1/, (accessed July 24, 2013).

Chapter 2

1. John Wesley, "A Plain Account of Christian Perfection as Believed and Taught by the Reverend Mr. John Wesley, From the Year 1725, to the Year 1777," in John Wesley, *The Works of John Wesley*, ed. Thomas Jackson (repr.; Grand Rapids, MI: Baker Books, 2002), 11:433 (henceforth, *Works*, Jackson).

2. J. W. Etheridge, *The Life of the Rev. Adam Clarke* (New York: Carlton and Porter, 1859), 189.

3. Ibid.

4. These statistics come from Roger Finke and Rodney Stark, *The Churching of America, 1776–2005: Winners and Losers in Our Religious Economy* (New Brunswick, NJ: Rutgers University Press, 2008), 56.

5. For more on the early Methodist approach to the "General Rules" and their contemporary relevance, see Kevin M. Watson, *A Blueprint for Discipleship: Wesley's General Rules as a Guide for Christian Living* (Nashville, TN: Discipleship Resources, 2009). For the text of the General Rules, see John Wesley, "General Rules," in *Works*, 9:69–73.

6. John Wesley, "General Rules," in *Works*, 9:69–70.

7. John Wesley, "A Plain Account of the People Called Methodists," in *Works*, 9:262.

8. Ibid.

9. Elaine A. Heath and Scott T. Kisker, *Longing for Spring: A New Vision for Wesleyan Community* (Eugene, OR: Cascade Books, 2010), 34.

10. Thomas R. Albin, "'Inwardly Persuaded': Religion of the Heart in Early British Methodism," in *"Heart Religion" in the Methodist Tradition and Related Movements*, ed. Richard B. Steele (Lanham, MD: Scarecrow Press, 2001), 45.

11. John Wesley, "A Plain Account of Christian Perfection," in *Works*, Jackson, 11:433.

12. *1798 Doctrines and Discipline*, 147.

13. Ibid., 147–48. Spelling and punctuation as in original.

14. For more detailed statistics on the miraculous growth of Methodism in America, see Finke and Stark, *The Churching of America*, 29, 56–57.

15. A variety of other explanations can also be seen to account for the numerical decline of Methodism over the last several decades. I am not making a formal academic argument here. Nevertheless, the decline of the class meeting is frequently included by historians of Methodism as at least a factor in the broader decline of American Methodism, if not the most important factor.

Chapter 3

1. John Wesley, "The Scripture Way of Salvation," in *Works*, 2:160.
2. John Wesley, "Thoughts upon Methodism," in *Works*, 9:527.
3. John Wesley, "The Principles of a Methodist Farther Explained," in *Works*, 9:227.
4. John Wesley, "General Rules," in *Works*, 9:70.
5. John Wesley, "Original Sin," in *Works*, 2:179–80.
6. John Wesley, "The One Thing Needful," in *Works*, 4:355.
7. John Wesley, "Original Sin," in *Works*, 2:183–84.
8. Ibid., 2:185.
9. John Wesley, "The Way to the Kingdom," in *Works*, 1:225.
10. John Wesley, "Justification by Faith," in *Works*, 1:189–90.
11. John Wesley, "Salvation by Faith," in *Works*, 1:120–21.
12. John Wesley, "The New Birth," in *Works*, 2:187.
13. Ibid.
14. John Wesley, "The Great Privilege of Those That Are Born of God," in *Works*, 1:431–32.
15. John Wesley, "The Witness of the Spirit, I," in *Works*, 1:274.
16. Charles Wesley, "O For a Thousand Tongues to Sing," in *The United Methodist Hymnal* (Nashville, TN: The United Methodist Publishing House, 2000), Hymn #57.
17. John Wesley, "The Scripture Way of Salvation," in *Works*, 2:158.
18. Ibid., 2:163.
19. Ibid., 2:160; emphasis added.
20. Ibid. 2:169; emphasis original.
21. John Wesley, Letter to Robert Carr Brackenbury, September 15, 1790; in *The Letters of John Wesley*, 8 vols., ed. John Telford (London: Epworth, 1931), 8:238.
22. John Wesley, "Minutes of Several Conversations between the Reverend Mr. John and Charles Wesley, and Others" (1763), in *Works*, 10:845.
23. John Wesley, *Journal* for August 25, 1763, in *Works*, 21:424.

Chapter 4

1. *1798 Doctrines and Discipline*, 148.
2. Roberts was also distressed by the Methodist Episcopal Church's compromise on slavery and the increased use of a pew rental system to finance increasingly ornate and expensive church buildings, which Roberts felt excluded the poor from Methodist churches. For a biography of B. T. Roberts and his wife, Ellen, see Howard A. Snyder, *B. T. and Ellen Roberts and the First Free Methodists*, abridged by Daniel V. Runyon (Indianapolis, IN: Light and Life Communications, 2011).
3. Peter Cartwright, *The Autobiography of Peter Cartwright* (New York: Carlton and Porter, 1857), 519–20.
4. Beverly Payne, afterword to *Waking to God's Dream: Spiritual Leadership and Church Renewal*, by Dick Wills (Nashville, TN: Abingdon, 1999), 109.
5. John Wesley, "Scripture Way of Salvation," in *Works*, 2:160.

Chapter 5

1. Dick Wills, *Waking to God's Dream: Spiritual Leadership and Church Renewal* (Nashville, TN: Abingdon, 1999), 47.
2. Ibid.
3. Ibid.
4. This section was shaped by my conversation with Dick Wills and reading his book, *Waking to God's Dream*, esp. 44–47.
5. It could well be that some of the people in the group are ready for deeper confession and accountability, such as was experienced in the early Methodist band meeting. See #7 of chapter 7 for a brief description of the band meeting.

Chapter 6

1. *1798 Doctrines and Discipline*, 136.
2. Ibid.
3. The best example of this was David Lowes Watson's Covenant Discipleship Groups, which were intended as a preliminary step toward a direct retrieval of the early Methodist class meeting. See David Lowes Watson, *Covenant Discipleship: Christian Formation through Mutual Accountability* (Nashville, TN: Discipleship Resources, 1991); *Forming Christian Disciples: The Role of Covenant*

Discipleship and Class Leaders in the Congregation (Nashville, TN: Discipleship Resources, 1991); and *Class Leaders: Recovering a Tradition* (Nashville, TN: Discipleship Resources, 1991). Steven W. Manskar has developed and advanced related themes in *Accountable Discipleship: Living in God's Household* (Nashville, TN: Discipleship Resources, 2000).

4. John Meunier, August 2, 2010 (9:04 p.m.), comment on Kevin M. Watson, "The Methodist Class Meeting for the 21st Century," *Vital Piety* (blog), August 2, 2010, http://vitalpiety.com/2010/08/02/the-methodist-class-meeting-for-the-21st-century-why-classes/).

5. An excellent resource on hearing from God is Dallas Willard, *Hearing God: Developing a Conversational Relationship with God* (Downers Grove, IL: Intervarsity, 2012).

6. Nick Weatherford, guest blog post, see http://vitalpiety.com/2011/02/22/hearing-from-a-21st-century-class-leader-part-2/ (accessed July 24, 2013).

Chapter 7

1. Peter Cartwright, *The Autobiography of Peter Cartwright*, 520.

2. Brian Mosley, "Shallow Small Group Bible Study—funny video from RightNowMedia.org", uploaded January 27, 2011, http://www.youtube.com/watch?v=NMyTMTmJU6E.

3. For a history of the band meeting and the role of communal formation in the early Methodist pursuit of holiness, see Kevin M. Watson, *Pursuing Social Holiness: The Band Meeting in Wesley's Thought and Popular Methodist Practice* (New York: Oxford University Press, 2014).

Chapter 8

1. Peter Cartwright, *The Autobiography of Peter Cartwright*, 519.

2. Ibid.

3. C. S. Lewis, *The Screwtape Letters* (New York: Harper Collins, 2001), 71.

Resources of Interest to Wesleyans

The Means of Grace by Andrew C. Thompson

In *The Means of Grace*, Andrew C. Thompson presents a clear and accessible explanation of the core tenets John Wesley instilled in the early Methodist movement. Each means of grace is drawn from biblical examples and paired with a framework to offer a real, practical model for a life marked by holy love and transformation. Wesley had a phrase for what it means to live faithfully as a disciple of Jesus: walking in the ways of God. Together, the means of grace demonstrate a Wesleyan pattern of discipleship and help us understand what are these ways of God. *Companion DVD available.*

The Band Meeting
by Kevin M. Watson and Scott T. Kisker
Coming in September 2017

In this companion to *The Class Meeting*, Kevin Watson teams up with Scott Kisker to write the definitive book on the most intimate small-group dimension of Wesley's strategy for Christian discipleship. History has now shown that the bands, as the smallest unit of early Methodist ministry model, was the most vital tool in Wesley's playbook for changing lives. Watson and Kisker show how this dynamic experience is relevant for today's church.

By Signs and Wonders by Stephen D. Elliott

As the church in North America trends toward a casual, cultural expression of Christianity, a surprising thing is happening. Instead of becoming more relevant, it's becoming less. As you'll see in these pages, the fastest-growing denominations and local churches around the world today are far more reliant on a strategy apart from friendship/lifestyle evangelism. That is the focus of this book, to provide laity and Christian leaders with a critically important insight in how to more effectively evangelize a lost and dying world. *Companion DVD available.*

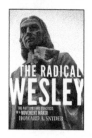

The Radical Wesley by Howard A. Snyder

How do you renew the church without destroying it? How do you gain an appreciation for the apostolic faith in a contemporary context? How do you touch people that the current tradition of the church doesn't touch? John Wesley had something to say about all these questions, and in *The Radical Wesley*, Howard Snyder skillfully takes Wesley's model and uses it as an outline for analysis of church renewal through the centuries.

Seedbed

OneBook.

THE EPIC OF EDEN
VIDEO STUDY GUIDE
by Sandra Richter

Let's be honest: it's just easier to study the New Testament. The pre-Jesus part of the Bible can seem so convoluted with lineages, stories, and laws that Jesus came to abolish. It's hard for us to make sense of it and see how it connects to God's bigger story at all. In *The Epic of Eden Video Study Guide* and *The Epic of Eden: Isaiah,* Dr. Sandra Richter jumps headlong into the Old Testament to clearly and powerfully communicate a history of God's redeeming grace, weaving together a story that runs from the Eden of the garden to the garden of the New Jerusalem. *Companion DVDs available.*

The Epic of Eden Video Study Guide • 12 Sessions
The Epic of Eden: Isaiah • 8 Sessions

DAILY-WEEKLY

Designed to be engaged by small groups, Sunday school classes, one-on-one discipleship approaches, and individual learners, the OneBook Daily-Weekly is a Bible learning resource for the long haul. *Companion DVDs available.*

The Gospel of John by Ben Witherington III
The Psalms—Part I by Brian D. Russell
The Letter to the Ephesians by Fredrick J. Long
The Book of Isaiah: Chapters 40–55 by John Oswalt
The Gospel of Mark by Brad Johnson
The Letter to the Romans by Ben Witherington III

Invitation by Brian Russell

How does Genesis connect to Revelation? What does Jesus have to do with the Old Testament? Why is Leviticus even in there? What is the big idea? *Companion DVD available.*

Onebook: Invitation *helps connect the dots for people as they discover the overarching story of God throughout the Scriptures. It's like putting a seminary education into the hands of the everyday layperson in the pews. My people are loving it. Great teaching by Brian Russell and great group discussion questions, which engage participants with the Word of God.*
—David Brasher, Pastor · First UMC, Bullard, Texas

Seedbed

seedbed.com

CPSIA information can be obtained
at www.ICGtesting.com
Printed in the USA
LVHW110756201118
597710LV00001B/1/P